DIALED IN

By Jim Ramos

Release Date: September 3, 2024
ISBN: 978-0-8307-8707-4
Price: $18.99
Trim Size: 5.5 x 8.25
272 pages
Format: Paperback

Religion/Christian Living/Men's Interests

advance reading copy
for promotional use only

What people are saying about ...

DIALED IN

"Our culture has taken direct aim at men and the crucial role they play in creating healthy families and thriving communities. The lie of 'toxic masculinity' devalues our men as protectors and providers and seeks to replace their God-given masculinity with passivity and mediocrity. Jim Ramos gets it. In *Dialed In*, he issues a clarion call for men to engage their masculinity at full capacity for the sake of the gospel. This book helps you take inventory of your masculine strength and grow into the man God created you to be. As the mother of two grown men and the grateful wife of a strong man, I am thrilled to see this book in print. We desperately need godly men to resume their place on the spiritual battlefield—and *Dialed In* offers a roadmap to get you there."

Heidi St. John, bestselling author and host of the *Off the Bench* podcast

"*Dialed In* 'is' Jim Ramos. This book is a loving call to action from a coach you always know is for you, but who's not afraid to challenge you to level up. He's extremely well-read, knows Scripture like the back of his hand, and tells great stories. Along the journey, you'll gain new knowledge about twenty of God's favorite character traits. Jim writes in a way that's both funny and serious, passionate and compassionate. By the time you finish, you'll feel dialed in—empowered to imitate the life, character, and conduct of our master, King Jesus. I hope you love this book as much as I did!"

Patrick Morley, PhD, bestselling author of 23
books, including *From Broken Boy to Mended Man*

"Jim Ramos has a way of 'messin with your business!' —in a good way. His straight talk to us, as men in an age of the soft and superficial, is refreshing. After every chapter, I found myself saying, 'Thanks, I needed that!' I needed this strong, practical, biblically sound 'calling up' to go for more, to be a man, to win for Jesus. *Dialed In* offers this and more. So grab some friends and go through this book together. You'll be glad you did."

Dr. Robert Lewis, author and founder
of Men's Fraternity and BetterMan

"If Satan can't get you to sin, he'll get you to settle for less—less of what God has for you; less of your spiritual inheritance; less promise, less power, less presence of God. Ramos calls us to not settle. He calls men to lay hold of their full inheritance, both now and in the world to come. I wholeheartedly recommend *Dialed In*. Don't settle for anything less."

Chris Harper, PhD, chief storyteller
and CEO of BetterMan

"We are living in a time and space where boys and men need a clear and compelling vision of what a godly man looks like. You are holding in your hands that vision. This book captures the characteristics that God uses to define manhood, and you will be inspired to be that man. When you choose to live as that man, your wife and children will thank you, and your legacy will shape the next generation. Let's get to it!"

Dave Wilson, co-host of the *Family Life Today* radio program and Detroit Lions chaplain for 33 seasons

"In Matthew 25, Jesus tells the story of a business owner and his employees. When the owner leaves three of his employees in charge of his investments, they achieve varying results. The employee who makes the greatest impact displays character, wisdom, and initiative. Upon returning, the owner honors the employee's excellence by saying, 'Well done, good and faithful servant.' In *Dialed In*, Jim Ramos opens us up to that man—the man who is faithful, good, and wise. Here's a game plan to build strong men, to strengthen a ministry to men, and to *become* that man. Well done, Jim; you are that man, and you're building more men like that—good and faithful servants."

Paul Louis Cole, president, Christian Men's Network

"There is a reason Jim Ramos connects with the hearts of men in both inspiring and provoking ways, and in *Dialed In* you experience why: Jim inspires men to become who God designed them to be and to move with God toward a grand role in the larger story. Men need advocates, teammates, and friends—those who will invite them up and into more in their relationship with God and others. This is a book for men who want to be challenged, invited, and encouraged."

Michael Thompson, founder and president of Zoweh and author of *The Heart of a Warrior* and *King Me*

JIM RAMOS

DIALED IN

Reaching Your Full
Capacity as a Man of God

DAVID C COOK
transforming lives together

DIALED IN
Published by David C Cook
4050 Lee Vance Drive
Colorado Springs, CO 80918 U.S.A.

Integrity Music Limited, a Division of David C Cook
Brighton, East Sussex BN1 2RE, England

DAVID C COOK® and related marks are registered trademarks of David C Cook.

The website addresses recommended throughout this book are offered as a resource
to you. These websites are not intended in any way to be or imply an endorsement
on the part of David C Cook, nor do we vouch for their content.

Library of Congress Control Number 2024933030
ISBN 978-0-8307-8707-4
eISBN 978-0-8307-8709-8

© 2024 James William Ramos
Published in association with the literary agency of Wordserve
Literary Group, Ltd., www.wordserveliterary.com.

The Team: Luke McKinnon, Kevin Scott, Gina Pottenger, Karissa Silvers, Susan Murdock
Cover Design: Brian Mellema

Printed in the United States of America
First Edition 2024

1 2 3 4 5 6 7 8 9 10

060624

FOR JAMES, DARBY, COLTON, AND FELIX

I am so pleased with the men you have become.
I am blessed to call each of you my "son."
Your unique gifts and abilities are enviable.
And I am one proud father.
You represent your name well.

But the most important name to represent is Jesus.
It is all about Him.
Never forget whom you serve.
Everything pales in comparison to
a life committed to Him.
Carry His legacy to your children!

I love each of you with all my soul.
You have what it takes!
I believe in you!
Win this life.

CONTENTS

When you look casually at this list of spiritual qualifications, you might conclude that Paul was exclusively outlining qualifications for men who serve in pastoral and teaching positions in the church. Not so! Rather, Paul was in essence saying to both Timothy and Titus that if a man wants to become a spiritual leader, that's great. Just make sure he is well on his way in becoming a man who is more and more measuring up to "the stature which belongs to the fullness of Christ." Paul then outlined how we can determine if he is this kind of man, using these specific qualities of maturity.

In other words, these qualities should be goals for every Christian man who is a Christ-follower.

—Dr. Gene Getz, *The Measure of a Man*

Let people feel the weight of who you are and let them deal with it.

—John Eldredge, *Wild at Heart*

INTRODUCTION

DIALING IT IN

"Dial it in" is a common phrase, but what does it mean? Those words take me back to a childhood tradition with my dad. Before each hunting season, we would use a three-step process to sight in our rifles, especially those with a newly mounted scope.

First, we boresighted the scope. This involved securing the firearm on a bench rest about fifty yards from the target, pulling the bolt out, and staring through the back end of the barrel until the barrel was centered on the target. Then, without moving the rifle, we used the vertical and horizontal dials on the scope to center the scope on the target, thus aligning the boresighted barrel to the newly mounted scope.

Once the gun was boresighted, we moved to the second step—putting bullets "on paper." This meant firing three shots at the target from fifty yards, checking where they hit the target, and then dialing it in, adjusting the scope, until the shots hit the desired mark.

Finally, we moved back to one hundred yards, shot several more rounds, and continued adjusting the scope until a three-shot group confirmed the gun was adequately dialed in. Dialing it in helps ensure that a rifle will perform effectively at specific distances. The shooter's accuracy, however, is another story.

A HEAVY BOOK

This book is admittedly heavy, not physically but functionally. It is meant to inspire you and convict you. It seeks to judge your manliness against the Word of God and leave you hungry for more—to become the man God created you to be. *Dialed In* is intended to catalyze change in your life, tipping the scales in your favor. You are about to redefine who you are, why you are here, and how you will impact the world. The world may reject the weightier you; it will ponder how to handle you at full capacity. And that is okay. Your job is to dial in the twenty qualities outlined in this book. It is the world's job to receive your gift. It is time for the world to feel the full weight of who you are—and deal with it.

In my book *Strong Men Dangerous Times: Five Essentials Every Man Must Possess to Change His World*, I identified five essential characteristics that separate men from mere males. Through this book you will notice a distinction I make between men and males. Genetically identical, they are vastly different. Here's how. Males are born. Men are made. Men are a product of function. Manhood is a choice. In other words, what makes a male a man is what he does far more than what he says. Males are the source of most of the world's problems. Men are the solution.

Dialed In is *Strong Men Dangerous Times* on steroids! It dials in those five characteristics of manhood with the twenty biblical qualifications of a spiritual leader found in two of the New Testament's Pastoral Epistles—1 Timothy and Titus. Having these qualifications should be the goal of every man.

Each chapter strategically ends with two opportunities. The Dial It In section is a set of study questions to be used with a group of men. It will help your group process each chapter together in the context of the Word of God and debrief any takeaways, questions, or challenges that manifested.

The fact that this book is in your hands is evidence that you are committed to living at full capacity. The ten Assessing Your Capacity questions at the end of each chapter are designed to assist you in identifying your masculine strengths and weaknesses so that you can dial in on specific areas to improve. They will help you inventory your strengths and growth areas. The goal of this book is to help you navigate to the best version of you. Use these assessments to identify your strengths and growth areas, then lean into becoming all that God has for you.

Keep a tally of your totals for the assessments in the appendix starting on page 273. After completing all of them, enter your scores on our website, meninthearena.org, and see how you compare with other men who have taken the *Dialed In* Assessment.

Each of the twenty qualifications for spiritual leaders found in the Pastoral Epistles are identified by single words or phrases, like "husband of one wife," "devout," "not addicted to wine," "just," and "not pugnacious." Some of these can be difficult to understand. Others are words that most of us never use in conversation today. When was the last time you used *prudent* in a sentence? Some phrases, quite frankly, are obscure and hard to understand. It took months to break down each one.

Each of the qualifications (the twenty chapter titles) has the following characteristics:

It is one word.

It is taken from the original Greek.

It is positive.

It is descriptive.

It translates the original biblical meaning into contemporary language.

It is masculine in nature.

Keep this in mind when you see each chapter title and subtitle.

A FULL-THROTTLE BOOK

You were made to function at full capacity. Anything less is a result of sin, whether by omission or commission. The goal of a dialed in man is to carry the weight of his life into eternity, completely spent and exhausted, with no potential left untapped and no gas in the tank.

This is not for the weak or soft-minded. It carries the weight of what a man firing on all cylinders looks like.

How do I know?

Our understanding of the dialed in man comes directly from the Pastoral Epistles in Scripture. 1 Timothy and Titus offer a road map for the highest levels of church leadership, which should be the goal of every man. In those letters, Paul listed twenty qualifications of the dialed in man. He used obscure words, some of which are obsolete in modern language, and he often used negative descriptive phrases. This book will help you sort out exactly what each qualification means.

Dialed In is an excellent resource for churches and Christian organizations in vetting potential spiritual leaders. Although it is a tool to measure a man's capacity, it should not be used as a legalistic device but as a guideline. Besides Jesus (Heb. 4:15), no man is perfect, and every man will fall short in at least one of the twenty categories. Be gracious.

Seek wisdom. Use discretion when vetting a man for a biblically qualified leadership position.

God made man on purpose, and that purpose is to live at full capacity. Look at our bodies. With testosterone pumping through our systems, we are larger than our beautiful female counterparts. We have more muscle mass. We are physically stronger. We are faster. We are laser-focused, compartmentalized-to-a-fault, task-oriented conquerors.

God made man to live at his highest level, both spiritually and physically—to carry the full weight of his masculine soul.

But the ability to carry any burden is in direct proportion to the carrier's capacity. Jesus said, "The thief comes only to steal and kill and destroy; I have come that they may have life, and have it to the full" (John 10:10 NIV). Jesus came to reclaim what the Enemy has stolen. What has he stolen?

Your capacity.

Your ability to operate as the best version of yourself.

Your urgency to dial it in.

We live in a world that says, "You do **you**." The problem? People don't mean it. What they mean is, "Conform to the world. Go with the flow. Blend in. Be fair. We are all the same." This is the Enemy's lie to rob the world of your greatest gift—you—the unapologetic version of you. God wants to put you on display for His glory. Anonymity is the great sin of the masculine soul.

The great apostle Paul wrote this about following cultural norms, "Do not conform to the pattern of this world, but be transformed by the renewing of your mind. **Then** you will be able to test and approve what God's will is—his good, pleasing and perfect will" (Rom. 12:2 NIV).

Welcome to *Dialed In*!

THE BLAMELESS MAN

Live above Reproach

An overseer, then, must be above reproach.

—1 Timothy 3:2

Prayer, meditation, and temptation make a minister.

—Martin Luther

TOP SHELF

I recently heard a story about two siblings who returned to clean up their childhood home after their parents died. As they sorted through their parents' belongings, keeping some things, selling others, and throwing away the rest, they entered the attic. Dingy and dusty, it was the junk drawer of the house, where their parents packed anything they wanted to save for a rainy day. You can fill in the blanks.

An antique appraiser was hired to make sure nothing of value was sold for too little or inadvertently thrown out. Among the throw-away and garage sale items was a sixteen-inch vase that looked like a genie could appear out of it at any moment and offer three wishes. The siblings never saw a genie, but their wish was granted when the appraiser said it could be worth as much as one million dollars!

The appraiser was wrong.

Way wrong.

The vase dated to the reign of Chinese emperor Qianlong, who reigned during the height of the Qing dynasty from 1735–1799. It bore the imperial seal and was most likely made for one of his imperial palaces. The siblings were even more amazed when the vase went into a twenty-minute bidding war and ultimately sold for seventy million dollars!

They had no idea that an obscure junk-room vase would change their lives. Can you imagine accidentally selling it at a garage sale for fifty cents, taking it to Goodwill, or using it for target practice? I don't know about you, but I'm not allowed to touch fragile things in our house. I break stuff. I'm that clumsy adult who grew up hearing his mom call him a bull in a china shop. I can imagine carrying that vase, bumping my shoulder on the door, launching the vase through the air, and staring in disbelief as it crashed into a thousand pieces!

Bill Pollard, former chairman and CEO of ServiceMaster, said, "Reputations are fragile. They must be handled with care like a valuable vase that if dropped can never quite be put together again."[1]

The Douay-Rheims 1582 version of the Bible uses "irreprehensible" in its translation of 1 Timothy 3:2. An irreprehensible man is one who handles his reputation with the utmost care, as you would a fragile vase of priceless value. We don't realize how fragile our reputations are and how easily they can crash and break into thousands of irretrievable pieces.

The night before I wrote this chapter, I took Shanna on a date. I asked her, "What positive word would you use to describe 'above reproach'?" After thoughtful consideration, she said, "Integrity." She's right. The "irreprehensible" (Douay-Rheims 1582) or "unrebukable"[2] man is a man of the highest integrity. He is blameless.

This chapter on being blameless is the first chapter on purpose. Without blamelessness, you are less than a man—a male masquerading as a man. Furthermore, you can be a great man without Jesus, but you can never be your best version. Chew on that for a while.

In 1 Timothy 3:2, Paul's listing "blameless" (NKJV) or "above reproach" as the first qualification was strategic. Jewish writers made lists in descending order from most prominent to least. The order in which they listed things in the Old and New Testaments is significant and can't be ignored. For example, who is listed first in both disciple lists? Peter, the most prominent of the Twelve (Matt. 10:2–4; Luke 6:14–16). Of course!

Guess who's last? Judas, the betrayer. Bummer, Judas!

Later in the book of Acts, we are introduced to a power couple named Aquila and Priscilla, also known as Prisca (Acts 18:2; 1 Cor. 16:19). Of the six times the couple is mentioned, Priscilla is listed *before* Aquila four times (Acts 18:18, 26; Rom. 16:3; 2 Tim. 4:19), which tells me she was a very significant team member in this dynamic duo.

Here's the bottom line: in both lists of overseer qualifications (1 Tim. 3:1–7 and Titus 1:5–9), being above reproach is strategically listed first. Why?

Because blamelessness is the summation of all the qualifications. In other words, living an unrebukable, irreprehensible life that is above reproach is the overarching theme of the dialed in man. It is the umbrella, if you will, covering the other nineteen qualities discussed in this book. It is the first and foremost quality, bar none.

SHOESTRING TACKLE

If you grew up playing sports, like me, you may have scars and nagging injuries from the old "glory days." I can clearly recall one high school football game. The funny thing is that I didn't play in it. Heck, I wasn't even there. My brother often talks about a time they played at Taft High School in California's Central Valley. Tom was tough but undersized at only 125 pounds in his senior year of high school.

I love how Tom tells the story. Taft High had a great running back in the late '80s—a big farm boy, who was fast, tough, and weighed 225 pounds. That is 100 pounds heavier than my brother. As a cornerback, Tom's primary responsibility was to defend the pass. When a corner makes a tackle on a run play, you know that something went bad in "the box" where the linemen and linebackers defend. Tom had a lot of tackling opportunities that infamous night when Morro Bay was drubbed by Taft.

The memorable play of this story came when that big back broke free on the outside and all he had between himself and the goal line was a skinny kid nicknamed by his teammates "the Stickman." Not the Hitman, the Stickman. The big back must've figured he would run right over the small defensive back rather than try to evade him. And he did. Tom's shoulder reminds him whenever he retells the story.

Ironically, just as the big back's cleat was pushing off Tom's chest, with the end zone in sight and only green grass between, my flailing little bro reached up, laid hold of the giant's shoestring, and tripped him up— just enough to prevent a touchdown.

A literal shoestring tackle!

It was an act of God. Tom would agree. His shoulder might not.

The Greek word often translated in 1 Timothy 3:2 as "above reproach" or "blameless" is *anepilemptos*, meaning "not to be laid hold of." What if the big back had tucked his shoestring into his cleats? What if he went for the juke instead of the truck? What if he taped over his laces? What if he wore stringless cleats (are those even a thing)? What if there were no string to lay hold of? That tiny shoestring was the big back's only point of vulnerability. But it was all the Stickman needed to trip him up.

Maybe he should have considered the words of the English Puritan preacher Richard Baxter, who said, "Be thoroughly acquainted with your temptations and the things that may corrupt you."[3] Maybe we should look at our spiritual shoes to double-check that they are double-knotted.

Shoestrings were the big back's weakness—his Achilles' heel. Remember the myth of Achilles, in which his mother dipped him in the river Styx, making his entire body invulnerable except for the part of his foot where she held him—the heel, which became Achilles' ultimate demise. The blameless man lives above reproach. He has no loose shoestrings, no Achilles' heel. He is a man of integrity.

The blameless man is, as N. J. D. White put it, "one against whom it is impossible to bring any charge of wrongdoing such as could stand impartial examination."[4] The *anepilemptos* man is not open to direct assault because he is "a man against whom no criticism can be made.... not open to attack, of a life which is not open to censure, of an art or technique which is so perfect that no fault can be found with it, of an agreement which cannot be broken."[5]

The idiom "chink in one's armor" refers to an area of vulnerability. It has traditionally been used to refer to a weak spot in a figurative suit of armor. The blameless man has no chink in his armor, no loose shoestrings, and no Achilles' heel. He lives above reproach. But no one lives in such a way without first having a plan.

As Matthew Henry described him, he

> must be blameless, he must not lie under any scandal; he must give as little occasion for blame as can be, because this would be a prejudice to his ministry and would reflect reproach upon his office.[6]

When it comes to being a man who lives above reproach, I think the saying "Failing to plan is planning to fail" summarizes it best. If you try to wing it, you may end up on the shoestring end of it.

Commit to living above reproach.

MODESTO MANIFESTO

November 3, 1948, was a big day for my ministry career. I wouldn't be born for another seventeen years, and my parents hadn't entered kindergarten yet. Thirty-one-year-old Billy Graham was ending a successful ministry run as an evangelist with Youth for Christ and launching a new ministry that would last almost six decades. In a rock-facade motel on S. Ninth Street in Modesto, California, members of Billy Graham's fledgling evangelistic team met to hash over the potential pitfalls of their profession.

As Christianity entered the postwar boom, Americans flocked to revivals. To guard against allegations of the abuse of money, sex, and power that had ruined evangelists before them, the passionate Graham team decided to take concrete steps to avoid the slightest air of controversy.

In that Modesto motel, Graham said, "Let's try to recall all the things that have been a stumbling block and a hindrance to evangelists in years past, and let's come back together in an hour and talk about it and pray about it and ask God to guard us from them."[7]

An hour later they compared their lists, which amounted to about fifteen items. High on all their lists were four overarching concerns. In *Just as I Am*, Graham recalled, "We pledged among ourselves to avoid any situation that would have even the appearance of compromise or suspicion. From that day on, I did not travel, meet, or eat alone with a woman other than my wife."[8]

Though they produced no written document, this "Modesto Manifesto" is the reason I've avoided ministry indiscretions that have taken out so many of my peers over the years. The manifesto included provisions for distributing money raised by offerings, avoiding criticism of local churches, working only with churches that support cooperative evangelism, and using official estimates of crowd sizes to avoid exaggeration. These policies would help Graham and his team avoid charges of financial exploitation and hucksterism. These are the four components of the manifesto:

1. We will never criticize, condemn, or speak negatively about others.
2. We will be accountable, particularly in handling finances, with integrity according to the highest business standards.
3. We will tell the truth and be thoroughly honest, especially in reporting statistics.
4. We will be exemplary in morals—clear, clean, and careful to avoid the very appearance of any impropriety.[9]

I've maintained my stance about being blameless around the opposite sex, but I did have the strangest hiccup many years ago. A seamstress volunteered to sew display covers that the fledgling Men in the Arena needed as backdrops for its display banners. My office was above a local coffee shop, and I told the seamstress I would meet her at the coffee shop and escort (wrong word) her to my office, where we would meet *once* with the door wide open.

The seamstress arrived just as the wife of a man in one of my men's groups was delivering flowers. Thinking nothing of it, I introduced them, conducted the brief meeting in my office, and carried on with my day.

What you need to know is that a major theme we constantly discuss within our small-group meetings is that married men ought to have healthy boundaries, or guardrails, with women who are not their wives. The next week the flower delivery woman's husband accosted me: "Thanks a lot! You sure got me into trouble. I came home from work last week to my wife saying, 'Guess who I saw at a coffee shop with another woman? Mr. Guardrails!'"

What a great reminder that even if your motives are pure, people are watching your every move. They don't do it out of spite. They do it because people are hungry to find men who really are passionate about Jesus and live their faith out boldly. Live a blameless life. Live above reproach.

STAY SHARP—STAY ALERT

Living in Oregon, the place where lumberjacks were invented, I love the old story of a young man who applied at a logging company during the 1800s. The foreman asked him if he could fell a tree with an axe. The young man walked over to a tree and felled it like an old pro.

The foreman hired him on the spot.

The next Monday, the young man outdid everyone else on the crew. But each day after that, he got slower and slower, until Friday, when he could barely cut one tree down. He went through all the motions, swinging his axe as hard as the day of his interview and repeating each powerful swing, but he barely made progress. Finally, the young man laid down his axe and sat on the ground in exhaustion, wondering what was wrong with him. The foreman put his hand on the young guy's shoulder and smiled. He said, "I know what is wrong. You've been so busy felling trees that you forgot to sharpen your axe. It is dull and worthless. You may as well be using a hammer. Now go sharpen your axe and keep it sharp from now on!"

I heard another story about an old lumberjack who, when asked how to chop down a tree, said, "Give me six hours to chop down a tree, and I will spend the first four sharpening the axe." I would add, give me a hundred years to serve God, and I will spend the first twenty sharpening my life—and every day after keeping it sharp.

Live above reproach—unrebukable, irreprehensible, blameless.

DIAL IT IN
Small-Group Exercises

1. The Greek word often translated as "above reproach" or "blameless" is *anepilemptos*, meaning "not to be laid hold of." What thoughts, insights, or takeaways do you have about this word?

2. Discuss this saying, which is often attributed to Billy Graham: "When wealth is lost, nothing is lost. When health is lost, something is lost. When character is lost, everything is lost."

3. Using a Bible app on your phone, look up 1 Timothy 3:2, 1 Timothy 5:7, and Titus 1:5b–7 in several translations. Which translation of *anepilemptos* resonates the most with you and why?

4. If Satan were to attack you in a way that would bring harm to your marriage and embarrassment to your family, where would he pounce (Gen. 4:7; John 10:10; 1 Pet. 5:8)?

5. Where do you need to implement 1 Thessalonians 5:22?

6. Read Matthew 6:12, James 5:16, and 1 John 1:9. Are there any unconfessed, secret sins that you need to bring into the light?

7. Have you just lied to us?

ASSESSING YOUR CAPACITY

For each of the ten assessment statements, rank yourself accordingly:

> (5) Strongly agree
>
> (4) Agree
>
> (3) Neither agree nor disagree
>
> (2) Disagree
>
> (1) Strongly disagree

Add up your total score at the bottom, then add the overall score in the appendix on page 274.

1. Nothing in my words or actions would cause people to doubt my integrity. _____

I have no secrets that, if found out, would embarrass those I love. _____

I can think of no one who might harbor bitterness toward me for my past actions. _____

I can think of no area where Satan might be setting a trap that would cause embarrassment to myself or those I love. _____

I have no hidden sins. _____

I have built accountability into my life with men who have my back. _____

I do not speak against someone or constructively criticize people if they are not there to hear it. _____

No one can bring a charge of wrongdoing against my character that could stand under impartial examination. _____

There are no loose ends, Achilles' heels, or other
things that could be used to lay hold of me.   ____

I handle my finances and business dealings with
impeccable integrity.   ____

TOTAL SCORE   ____

THE SERVANT

Wear the Servant's Towel

Faithful servants never retire. They serve faithfully as long as they're alive. You can retire from your career, but you will never retire from serving God.

—Rick Warren, *The Purpose Driven Life*

Having joined the expedition to protect his father, Kermit worked ... harder than most, spending such long hours in the river that his shoes literally rotted off his feet.

—Candice Millard, *The River of Doubt*

RIVER OF DOUBT

The River of Doubt is Candice Millard's masterful account of Theodore Roosevelt's expedition down an unknown Amazon tributary, now known as the Roosevelt River, or Rio Roosevelt, with his second son, Kermit. It is one of the greatest adventure stories I've ever read. And it is true! I

believe that the adventure was ultimately the catalyst that led to Teddy
Roosevelt's death six years later at only sixty years old.

Kermit, who joined the expedition to ensure safe passage for his
father, is the unspoken hero of the book. The elder Roosevelt started the
journey as a fifty-five-year-old man. He had only one strong leg because
of a trolley accident twelve years earlier in 1902[1]. That, combined with a
bullet lodged in Roosevelt's chest from a 1912 assassination attempt, left
him with compromised health.[2]

Knowing this, before leaving New York, Roosevelt packed his usual
lethal dose of morphine: "Because one never knows what is going to happen.... I always meant that, if at any time death became inevitable, I would
have it over with at once, without going through a long-drawn-out agony
from which death was the only relief."[3]

His prevailing thought was that "no man has any business to go on
such a trip unless he will refuse to jeopardize the welfare of his associates
by any delay caused by a weakness or ailment of his. He must go forward,
if necessary, on all fours, until he drops. Only those are fit to live who do
not fear to die."[4]

Weeks before their rescue, Roosevelt cut his leg badly while saving two
canoes from smashing into each other, which led to a bacterial infection in
his weaker leg. He soon became so ill with malaria and the bacterial infection that he could no longer sit up. Surrendering to his fate, he said to the
expedition leader and his son, "Boys, I realize that some of us are not going
to finish this journey. Cherrie, I want you and Kermit to go on. You can get
out. I will stop here" (and die by a lethal dose of morphine).[5]

But staring at his father lying in his sweat, prone and unable to sit up,
Kermit refused his father's request. "Whatever it took, whatever the cost,"
wrote Millard, "he would not leave without Roosevelt."[6] And that is exactly

what happened. Kermit carried and canoed his father, compromising nothing to get him safely home, and Kermit succeeded. Six years later, Roosevelt died in his sleep at sixty due to complications from those events.

Kermit's actions are some of the most impressive feats of service I've ever read. Almost. The greatest act of service is articulated in Romans 5:8: "But God demonstrates His own love toward us, in that while we were yet sinners, Christ died for us."

But God.

The night before Jesus' crucifixion the disciples gathered for a meal, just moments before Judas's betrayal, but God washed the traitor's feet anyway—the same feet that would run to those who would kill Jesus. In this context, John 13:12–15 is one of the greatest examples in the Bible of a man who lives at full capacity:

> So when He had washed their feet, and taken His garments and reclined at the table again, He said to them, "Do you know what I have done to you? You call Me Teacher and Lord; and you are right, for so I am. If I then, the Lord and the Teacher, washed your feet, you also ought to wash one another's feet. For I gave you an example that you also should do as I did to you."

Whatever it took, whatever the price, Jesus would not leave the earth without serving humanity—even His enemies—at the cost of His life. And in so doing He gave us an example to follow:

> Have this attitude in yourselves which was also in Christ Jesus, who, although He existed in the form

of God, did not regard equality with God a thing to be grasped, but emptied Himself, taking the form of a bond-servant, and being made in the likeness of men. (Phil. 2:5–7)

Ray Pritchard rightly observed, "We could easily overlook this verse in our haste to get to the list of qualifications of spiritual leaders. That would be a great mistake because it reveals an overlooked ingredient of leadership: godly leaders must want the job."[7]

Being a servant is what sets a God-fearing man apart from a poser. A man and everything around him will change once he chooses to move from being an anonymous observer in the church bleachers to being a player in the game. Joe Myall is a friend, one of my youth ministry volunteers from the '90s and a monitor on our thousands-strong Men in the Arena Facebook group. At over seventy years old, he got a Men in the Arena tattoo on his upper arm. Our brand is on his arm! When I saw it for the first time, he told me, "This is not about the organization, Men in the Arena, but a reminder for me to stay out of the anonymous bleachers and stay in the arena—the fight."

Jesus represents everything we ask men to do. The dialed in man imitates the Lord Jesus Christ and puts on the servant's towel.

THE PREREQUISITE

You may be wondering about the title of this chapter, which is based on 1 Timothy 3:1—"It is a trustworthy statement: if any man aspires to the office of overseer, it is a fine work he desires to do"—especially because this verse does not specifically address a qualification of leadership.

Or does it?

In school, I had to take certain classes to qualify for others. These were called *prerequisites*. Algebra 1 preceded Geometry. Geometry qualified me for Algebra 2. After that, I was qualified for Trigonometry, then Calculus. You get the point.

Being a servant is not technically listed as one of the qualifications for a spiritual leader, yet it is the prerequisite of them all. Just as being blameless is the overarching theme of the twenty qualifications, being a servant is the prerequisite for the dialed in man. If a man is not willing to engage, serve, and humbly be put on display, then—guess what?

He won't be.

In that sense, this is a critical chapter. Living at full capacity starts with the choice to put on the servant's towel.

DESIRE AND DRIVE

A closer look at 1 Timothy 3:1 reveals an inherent quality of the dialed in man: "It is a trustworthy statement: if any man aspires to the office of overseer, it is a fine work he desires to do."

Not only does he have the *internal desire* to be his best version, but he also has the *external drive* to back it up. This twofold quality—desire and drive—is what sets him apart from those who dream about greatness but never act on their desire. At some point, a man must turn his dreams into drives, his aspirations into actions, his words into works.

Years ago, while welcoming students to youth group, I was alarmed by a girl who showed up with what looked like a road rash all over her face and legs. The fresh blood was still shining off her mangled face and knees.

"Brianna, what happened to you?"

Brianna, as a freshman, was the star of her varsity track team, specializing in the two-hundred-meter dash. With bloodshot eyes, she shared how when she leaned her chest as far over the finish line as she could, she lost her balance and tumbled face-first into the track. At the time, her school had a dirt track, and because she couldn't get her hands in front of her, her face and knees skid across the gravel!

Brianna's brutal story is a brilliant word picture. The word *aspires* in 1 Timothy 3:1 is a translation of the Greek word *orego*, a rare word that appears only here and two other places in the New Testament. One of those places is 1 Timothy 6:10, which says, "For the love of money is a root of all sorts of evil, and some by **longing for it** have wandered away from the faith and pierced themselves with many griefs." *Orego* is found again in Hebrews 11:16: "But as it is, they **desire** a better country, that is, a heavenly one."

Desire, as translated from *orego*, literally means "to reach or stretch out to obtain a certain goal."[8] It is pictured as an external act, like stretching with all one's might over an imaginary finish line. It describes someone who is taking the right steps to become an overseer. It paints a picture of a man who is doing something, rather than simply talking about something.

The apostle Peter addressed the right steps when he wrote, "Therefore, I exhort the elders among you ... shepherd the flock of God among you, exercising oversight not under compulsion, but voluntarily, according to the will of God" (1 Pet. 5:1–2). The greatest leaders model their lives after the greatest servant—Jesus Christ. Unless a man is willing to act like Jesus, to take steps to serve others, he is not fit for spiritual leadership.

My life and marriage changed when I committed to "out-love" and "out-serve" Shanna. It was the day I chose to stretch myself, to reach ahead of others, to lead the way. It was the day I became a man. It was the day I decided to put on the servant's towel. I was thirty years old.

The second word I want to highlight in 1 Timothy 3:1 is *desires*, from the Greek word *epithumeo*, which means "a passionate compulsion." In contrast to *orego*, this verb refers to an *internal* feeling, passion, or desire. It is the attitude that precedes the actions. It is the desire that precedes the direction.

Taken together, *orego* and *epithumeo* describe the man who internally desires more for his life and is driven to pursue his dreams with external action.

This man desires to wear the servant's towel, then puts it on and serves others. Men who are operating at full capacity are servants. They wear the servant's towel, not the king's regalia. They are the greatest servants in the church.

Saint Francis of Assisi once said, "We must never desire to be above others, but, instead, we must be servants and subject to every human creature for God's sake."[9]

A servant leader is one who wears the servant's towel and actively serves.

SAVED TO SERVE OR SERVE TO BE SAVED?

The question arises, "Are we saved to serve, or do we serve to be saved?"

Yes, to both.

I heard about a man who was hiking in Alaska's Chugach Mountains when a violent snowstorm hit. At about 250 miles long, the Chugach Mountains are the northernmost part of the Pacific Coast Ranges on the western edge of North America. They receive more snowfall than anywhere else in the world, with an annual average of over eight hundred inches a year!

The blizzard hit the man so fast that he couldn't make it back to camp, which he knew was only a short distance away. Because the wind was so strong, he became snow-blind. In the dark of the night, he burrowed into a snowbank to ride it out, hoping merely to survive the night. Exhausted, with frozen appendages, he resolved to die.

Then he heard it—a faint cry, like the whimpering of a puppy. He crawled out of his ice cave and called out into the night. Sure enough, it was a young pup who got separated from his mother and got lost in the storm. The pup was freezing to death, so the man started vigorously rubbing the dog's body, trying to keep its blood circulating and save its life. He warmed the pup with his breath and continued rubbing the dog through the night.

The next day, scouts from the village found both the man and the puppy—cold but alive. They determined that by feverishly working to keep the freezing pup alive during the night, the man had saved his own life as well.

Ephesians 2:8–10 is one of my life verses: "For by grace you have been saved through faith; and that not of yourselves, it is the gift of God; not as a result of works, so that no one may boast. For we are His workmanship, created in Christ Jesus for good works, which God prepared beforehand so that we would walk in them."

We are saved to serve, and, in serving, our lives are saved and given a purpose for living. Get out of the bleachers and into the arena. Gird your loins with the servant's towel.

DIAL IT IN
Small-Group Exercises

1. Why do you think 1 Timothy 3:1 is the primary reference used for this chapter?

2. What do *aspires* and *desires* mean in 1 Timothy 3:1? How are they different from each other? How are they similar?

3. Discuss Rick Warren's famous quote, "Faithful servants never retire. They serve faithfully as long as they're alive. You can retire from your career, but you will never retire from serving God."[10]

4. How did Jesus model servanthood? What Bible passages can you think of that reference Jesus as a servant? Consider Matthew 20:26–28 and Philippians 2:5–7.

5. What are some things you can do to follow Jesus' example in John 10:11?

6. Consider Jesus the night before His crucifixion. He wore the servant's towel and washed the disciples' feet. Keeping in mind Jesus' example, who is worthy to be served? Consider John 13:5–10, 15, 21.

ASSESSING YOUR CAPACITY

For each of the ten assessment statements, rank yourself accordingly:

(5) Strongly agree

(4) Agree

(3) Neither agree nor disagree

(2) Disagree

(1) Strongly disagree

Add up your total score at the bottom, then add the overall score in the appendix on page 275.

1. I find true joy in serving others.   _____

My family would say that I am a willing servant.   _____

I have a circle of friends who feel safe confiding in me.   _____

I believe in finding a local fellowship of believers and
  making a commitment to them.   _____

I have served in numerous roles in my church or com-
  munity.   _____

I am saved by grace, but God has a mission and plans
  for my life.   _____

I am often asked to serve in various capacities.   _____

I believe that Christians are saved to serve.   _____

The leaders of my church know my name.   _____

A man should look more for ways to serve his church
  than for ways his church can serve him.   _____

TOTAL SCORE   _____

THE WITNESS

Missionary or Mission Field?

While our generation is screaming for answers, too many Christians are stuttering.

—Howard Hendricks

No one is likely to receive Christ through you who will not receive you first.

—Joseph Aldrich, *Gentle Persuasion*

COACH WITNESS

A few years ago, I noticed one of my football players from 1993–1995 had started interacting with our online group, which was intriguing since Grant was from a strict cultish background. I learned that after his parents' divorce, everything had crumbled. His parents left their church, and Grant was left trying to figure it out. Along the way, he found Jesus. While he was visiting my hometown a few years back, we connected for a cup of coffee. He wasn't the short, stocky, curly-haired noseguard who was missing his front teeth that I remembered. Instead, this fit, slightly graying, handsome man (with all his teeth) shared how he found Jesus behind a trash dumpster while working as a landscaper.

I listened in amazement.

One thing he shared stood out. While seeking out the truth, he reflected on people who possessed an authentic faith, and I came to mind. He relayed something I still don't remember: "You used to open the weight room for us, then go into the coach's office and read your Bible while we lifted, and I never forgot how real your faith was to you."

God wove me into Grant's story, and Grant is an active part of our ministry today.

Someone once said, "To many, you may be the only Jesus they will ever see." We live in a world that desperately needs Jesus, and sadly, as Howard Hendricks once said, "While our generation is screaming for answers, too many Christians are stuttering."[1] This chapter is critical for any man who wishes to live dialed in. In a world that tries to push men around, it is time for men to push back. Don't shrink back from who you are (Heb. 10:39). Push until they feel the full weight of who you are.

Become a missionary on the earth's vast mission field.

MISSIONARY OR MISSION FIELD?

Before Shanna and I fell in love and got married, she was one of my volunteers with Youth for Christ and Campus Life. I knew she was a special woman when, during a staff meeting, she said something I've never forgotten: "You are either a missionary or a mission field."

That was in 1991. She had a ring on her finger a year later. Today, she still embodies that mantra in her career as a flight attendant. The airline industry is unique in that crew members don't work the same shift, as in other jobs, but every flight has a different crew. She has never flown with the same crew twice, which means she must get to know different crew members each time she flies. She is paid to be a flight attendant but lives to be a missionary, rarely landing without knowing her fellow flight attendants' names, faith stories, and prayer needs.

How does she do it? She simply asks them about their lives. They gladly share. People are selfish, yes, but they are also hurting and desperate to share their stories with a caring heart. It is a gift and a commitment to be a missionary, not a mission field. Shanna has a tremendous reputation with her coworkers.

1 Timothy 3:7 says that an overseer "must have a good reputation with those outside the church, so that he will not fall into reproach and the snare of the devil."

The original Greek words for "good reputation" are *marturian* ("witness") and *kalen* ("good"), which, when put together, mean "good report" or "an excellent testimony"[2] or "witness, evidence, testimony, reputation."[3] We get the word *martyr* from *marturian*. I love what the great New Testament scholar N. T. Wright once said, "When God wants to sort out the world, ... he doesn't send in the tanks. He sends in the meek, the broken, the justice hungry, the peacemakers, the pure-hearted and so on."[4]

God doesn't need men to steamroll others with their astute apologetics. He is looking for people, like Shanna, to build His reputation through their exemplary lives. But a good reputation takes years to build, and it starts with an authentic life.

Let your reputation precede you. As German poet Heinrich Heine is believed to have said, "You show me your redeemed life and I might be inclined to believe in your Redeemer."

The dialed in man displays his full posture to a lost world that needs Jesus. He is a tactical missionary. That is the beauty of missionaries. They strategically embed themselves into their world. They are patient. They look for the perfect opportunity to be salt, light, and witnesses for Jesus. They are not transient, like so many today, but sink deep roots. Like Job, they believe, "I will die in my own house, my days as numerous as the grains of sand. My roots will reach to the water, and the dew will lie all night on my branches" (Job 29:18–19 NIV).

Are you a missionary or a mission field?

DIAMONDS IN THE ROUGH

I once read a story about a wealthy merchant who was seeking to buy a very special diamond to add to his collection. (You know you're rich if you have a diamond collection!) Hearing of such a diamond in the States, he flew on his jet from Holland to New York, where the store had tasked one of the top diamond experts on the planet with closing the transaction and sealing the deal. After hearing the diamond expert's boring discourse on the perfect technical details of the diamond, he chose *not* to purchase it.

Before he boarded his jet back to Holland, the store owner asked, "Do you mind if I show you that stone once more?" The Dutchman agreed.

Without repeating anything the expert had mentioned, the store owner gently took the stone in hand, stared at it with great awe, and described its unique beauty in a way that revealed how this stone stood out from any stone he'd ever laid eyes on. The Dutch collector then bought it immediately. Tucking it gingerly into his suit pocket, he commented, "Sir, I wonder why you were able to sell me that diamond when your expert salesman could not?"

The owner replied, "My salesman is one of the top experts on diamond quality in the world. He knows more about them from a technical standpoint than anyone I have ever met, and I pay him a lot of money to do so. But I would gladly double his salary if I could add one thing to him that he lacks. You see, sir, he *knows* diamonds very well. But I *love* them."

Building a good reputation among those outside the church is not about knowing how to share your faith. It isn't even about wanting to share your faith or obeying the biblical command to preach the gospel to all nations (Mark 16:15). It is simply about loving Jesus so much that you will do anything to see a dying world come to know Him. Missionaries share out of an overflow of their love for God more than from their knowledge of Him.

Being a witness and building a solid Christian reputation starts with those in closest proximity to you (such as your immediate family), then your neighbors, coworkers, and beyond. Joseph Aldrich might have been thinking about diamonds when he wrote, "No one will receive Christ through you who will not receive you first. You are the message."[5]

Diamonds are mined from the earth with great effort. Being a man with a good reputation, *marturian kalen*, takes time and tactics.

Commit to being a missionary, not a mission field.

WHAT KIND OF NEIGHBOR ARE YOU?

John Locke was an English philosopher and physician, widely regarded as one of the most influential thinkers of the Enlightenment. He is credited with the statement, "To love our neighbor as ourselves is such a truth for regulating human society, that by that alone one might determine all the cases in social morality."

As a new follower of Jesus, I took Jesus' words to heart: "This is the great and foremost commandment. The second is like it, 'You shall love your neighbor as yourself'" (Matt. 22:38–39). Loving God was easy for me, as a new believer, to conceptualize, but who exactly was my neighbor? As a new Christian, taking Scripture at face value, I determined that my neighbors were ... wait for it ... those people living near me—immediate family and literal neighbors.

Simple.

There's no better way to be a missionary to our world than to start with those who watch our lives in real time—our neighbors and those who live in proximity to us. They see if I keep up my yard. They see me playing (or not playing) with my kids in the yard. They hear me yelling at my wife and kids. They notice if I take my trash cans in or leave them on the street until next week. They notice whether I hang Christmas lights and how long I leave them up after the holidays. They are best positioned to judge whether my faith is all that I claim it is. My reputation increases or diminishes in the front yard. You can tell a lot about your neighbors without even trying.

You can be a missionary or a mission field. Richard Whately is often paraphrased as observing, "A man is called selfish not for pursuing his good, but for neglecting his neighbor's."

Over the years I have seen many neighbors come and go, learned their names, mowed their lawns, watched several come to faith in Jesus, and baptized some simply because I was a proactive, good neighbor. In the days of Jesus, a close extended family was the norm, with children, parents, and grandparents often in the same home for generations. People stuck around. Even Jesus, in His lifetime, never ventured more than one hundred miles from His home. In ancient times, adult children often built their homes over the flat roofs of their parents' homes. Everyone knew who the good, bad, and ugly neighbors were.

Jesus reminded us in Matthew 5:13–16:

> You are the salt of the earth; but if the salt has become tasteless, how can it be made salty again? It is no longer good for anything, except to be thrown out and trampled under foot by men.

> You are the light of the world. A city set on a hill cannot be hidden; nor does anyone light a lamp and put it under a basket, but on the lampstand, and it gives light to all who are in the house. Let your light shine before men in such a way that they may see your good works, and glorify your Father who is in heaven.

What kind of neighbor are you? Better yet, what kind of reputation do you have in your neighborhood? How many of your neighbors know you? How many know you follow Jesus?

It isn't hard to be a missionary to those around you. You just need to be tactical. Instead of being our best selves on Sunday and being anonymous in our neighborhoods, maybe we should learn the names of our neighbors, collect their cell numbers in case of an emergency, and build solid reputations as Christian neighbors.

One bad neighbor I had is especially memorable. He rented a house adjacent to ours for a season. When he moved out, the homeowners—our friends and not practicing believers—had to replace all the carpets and paint the house! This not only hurt his reputation but also damaged God's witness through his pathetic behavior. Who was this bad neighbor?

A local music minister!

You are either a missionary or a mission field.

HOLY HUDDLES

The second part of 1 Timothy 3:7 is significant to our discussion, and I want to close this chapter with it: "So that he will not fall into reproach and the snare of the devil." Early on in my ministry career, I noticed that key laymen acted and spoke like men who were more passionate about Jesus than pastors—and often stuck around the church longer! Being a pastor myself, this troubled me. After careful consideration, I determined why that was and resolved never to be that man.

First, the average pastor doesn't sink deep roots in a community the way a layman does. Pastors tend to be transient, living in multiple communities during their career. When I visit the two churches I worked in, the pastors are all long gone, but the laypeople remain. It is their church. They are more committed to it. Second, a minister is paid to do what laymen do just because they love Jesus. Third, the layman is compelled to build his reputation among nonbelievers because he works with them every day! The pastor is locked in his holy office and interacts mostly with his holy congregation and inanimate computer screen. If he isn't purposeful about building his reputation outside the church, he is like a fifteen-year-old homeschooled kid who is at the top of his class, which is graded on a curve! Pastors typically don't have to compete, interact, or learn how to be a missionary in the vast mission field. The closest they get to nonbelievers is greeting some of the men on Sunday. This leads to a false sense of pride, which is a snare of the devil.

We must be tactical about climbing out on the limb where the fruit is hanging. Remember, you are either a missionary or a mission field.

DIAL IT IN
Small-Group Exercises

1. What are your thoughts on the idea that you are either a missionary or a mission field?

2. Howard Hendricks said, "While our generation is screaming for answers, too many Christians are stuttering."[6] Are you being won over by other philosophies and beliefs, or are you focused on winning others to Christ?

3. Read Leviticus 19:18, Mark 12:31, and 1 Timothy 3:7. How are you building a good reputation with your neighbors?

4. What are your thoughts about Matthew 5:14–16?

5. What would your neighbors say about you, based on what they see from across the street?

6. Where has your life become a holy huddle as you've turned away from your needy world?

7. Where do you need to repair a damaged reputation?

ASSESSING YOUR CAPACITY

For each of the ten assessment statements, rank yourself accordingly:

(5) Strongly agree

(4) Agree

(3) Neither agree or disagree

(2) Disagree

(1) Strongly disagree

Add up your total score at the bottom, then add the overall score in the appendix on page 276.

1. My neighbors think well of me. _____

Those who know me best respect me the most. _____

People who know me would tell you that my word is
my bond. _____

I am known as a man with impeccable integrity. _____

I have no enemies. _____

My life is well-ordered, without a lot of unfinished
projects. _____

I am always on time to do the things I've committed to. _____

I treat all people with respect and dignity, regardless
of age, gender, politics, or race. _____

People are comfortable putting me in responsible
positions. _____

I never use unwholesome talk. _____

TOTAL SCORE _____

4

THE CALM MAN

Keep Calm and Carry On

Timid men ... prefer the calm of despotism to the tempestuous sea of liberty.

—Thomas Jefferson

Anyone can hold the helm when the sea is calm.

—Publilius Syrus

KEEP CALM AND CARRY ON

I was the speaker at a high school summer camp a few years ago on the camp's theme, "Keep Calm until the Kingdom Comes." At the time "Keep calm" was a wildly popular saying, and I didn't understand why until I discovered that it originated in Europe in 1939 during the events leading up to World War II.

Germany, under the leadership of Adolf Hitler, made the Pact of Steel alliance with Italy, annexed Austria, signed a nonaggression pact with the

Soviet Union, attacked Czechoslovakia and Poland, and allied itself with Japan. War with England was imminent. England was still recovering from World War I with Germany, and the English people were overcome with fear of an imminent attack. By September, England and France declared war against Nazi Germany, which is now called the "Phony War" because nothing occurred until Germany's bombing of London in 1940.

Threatened with widely predicted mass air attacks and public uneasiness, the English government ordered the mass production of 2.5 million posters with the saying "Keep Calm and Carry On" to raise public morale and evoke the British reputation for keeping a stiff upper lip when faced with adversity.

But the posters were rarely displayed and ultimately forgotten once bombs started falling on London. In 2000, the old posters were discovered in a bookstore in England, and the saying rapidly grew in global popularity.[1]

Keep calm and carry on.

ANGER MANAGEMENT ISSUES

Writing a book is a team effort. If it weren't so, authors wouldn't include an acknowledgments page. By the time this book got to the retailer, who ultimately sold it to you, it needed an author (yours truly), editor, copy editor, proofreader, cover designer, publisher, marketing team, and distributors. We spent many hours over the course of a year discussing the twenty chapters in this book, the perfect word choices, and the assessment statements at the end of each chapter.

For this chapter, we originally chose "The Patient Man" as the perfect description of the man who is "not quick-tempered" (Titus 1:7). Then I discovered the Greek word behind this phrase, *orgilos*, and everything changed.

There are two Greek words for anger. There is *thumos*, which is the anger that quickly blazes up and just as quickly subsides, like a fire in straw. There is *orgē*, the noun connected with *orgilos*, and it means ingrained anger. It is not the anger of the sudden blaze, but the wrath continually fed to keep it alive. A blaze of anger is an unhappy thing, but this long-lived, purposely maintained anger is still worse. Those who nourish their anger against another person are not fit to be office-bearers of the Church.[2]

Orgilos reminds me of the water kettle we use. My preferred drink, the café Americano, requires pouring a double shot of espresso over boiling water. The water must boil, which happens at exactly 212 degrees Fahrenheit. The Chinese describe the five stages of boiling water as shrimp eyes, crab eyes, fish eyes, a rope of pearls, and a raging torrent.[3] Similarly, *orgilos* describes the person who is always simmering, just a few degrees from boiling.

The autoignition point of paper is 451 degrees Fahrenheit. Ironically, when Ray Bradbury was asked about the subject of his 1953 dystopian classic, *Fahrenheit 451*, he said, "Well, Hitler, of course. When I was 15, he burned the books in the streets of Berlin. Then along the way, I learned about the libraries in Alexandria burning 5,000 years ago.... And if it could happen in Alexandria, if it could happen in Berlin, maybe it could happen somewhere up ahead, and my heroes would be killed."[4]

History proves that Hitler was always near boiling or like paper ready to combust. This is *orgilos*. Titus 1:7 is a warning to be vigilant against harboring anger just below the surface. *Orgilos* is "ingrained anger." It has been described as "long-lived, purposely maintained anger" frequently with the intention to take revenge. It is less sudden in its rise than *thumos*—an angry outburst—but more lasting in nature.[5]

Orgilos reminds me of something I've seen duck hunting. I rarely duck hunt alone, and during the slower moments when the ducks aren't moving, the temptation is to talk to my hunting buddies—usually my sons. The assumption is that someone is still watching for ducks, but that is often not true. It is when our guards are down that a solo duck will sneak into the decoy spread and quickly discover its mistake: "These aren't my buddies! Oh no! Stay calm. Don't appear nervous. Paddle fast. I need to get out of here ASAP!"

The poor waterfowl tries to outwardly maintain its cool while frantically paddling out of the decoy spread. On the surface, it looks poised and calm, but there's a torrent under the surface as it tries to get out of shotgun range. But you already know how that story ends.

Keep calm and paddle on!

The quick-tempered, or *orgilos*, man is in a constant state of inner turmoil. Those closest to him know it and walk on eggshells around him. Maybe you know this guy. Maybe you **are** this guy! He struggles to have friends because when something triggers an eruption—friendship over. Those who do remain loyal to him either stay strategically outside his inner circle or become codependents. He must free himself from the undercurrent of *orgilos*.

Keep calm and carry on.

YOU'RE DRIVING TOO SLOW

A children's pastor once shared an alarming, yet hilarious, story about an event he witnessed between two children. He found them fighting during

Sunday school, separated them, and said, "When I come back, I want to see that your angry eyes have changed."

But when he returned, the little boy across the room facing the pastor had fried-egg eyes, wide open, with a horrified look on his face. When the pastor turned to the boy behind him, the little guy had his middle finger raised toward the other boy in an obvious act of nonverbal aggression.

My pastor friend asked, "Do you know what you are doing?"

"Yes," the leering child responded, as he stared, his finger still in the air, focused at the wide-eyed boy across the room.

"Can you tell me what that middle finger means?"

Staring angrily, the seven-year-old said, "It means you're driving too slow!"

I wonder if he learned about driving too slowly from his dad! I bet he learned the gesture from a man whose anger was just below the surface waiting to erupt. Does that guy sound familiar? I love the Chinese proverb, "If you are patient in one moment of anger, you will escape a hundred days of sorrow." When was the last time someone or something made you angry and set you off? Proverbs 14:17 warns that "a quick-tempered man acts foolishly, and a man of evil devices is hated."

We've deservedly picked on Hitler in this chapter, but I see anger bubbling beneath the surface of many great leaders, since passion often fuels men of great vision. Gene Getz's description of *orgilos* as "passionate" affirms this connection between passion and anger.[6]

This discussion reminds me of a story about a woman who was bitten by a rabid dog. After examining her, the doctor informed her that she had waited too long to get help and that her survival looked dim. He recommended that she prepare a will. She borrowed his pen and notepad and wrote so much for so long that the doctor finally said, "That sure is a long will you're making."

She snorted, "Will, nothing! I'm making a list of all the people I'm going to bite!"

Her anger was just below the surface and ready to boil. Saint Francis de Sales is often credited with writing, "Never be in a hurry; do everything quietly and in a calm spirit. Do not lose your inner peace for anything whatsoever, even if your whole world seems upset."

Easier said than done. Keep calm and carry on.

KEEP CALM AND KILL A PYTHON

I'm not known as a calm man. It is a growth area I identified while writing this chapter. If you don't believe me, I can show you the four blood pressure medicines I take daily! My blood pressure has really skyrocketed on the many occasions when I've had to do what I call the "rattlesnake dance," jumping straight up in the air and dancing around a rattlesnake as I try to avoid getting bit. *Calm* is the last word I'd use to describe those moments, which is why the next story was so inspiring.

A shiver went up my spine when I heard a popular sermon illustration about the supposed instructions given to men planning to serve in the Peace Corps in Brazil for what they should do if they encountered a hungry anaconda:

1. If you're attacked by an anaconda, do not run. The snake is faster than you are.
2. Lie flat on the ground. Put your arms tight against your sides, your legs tight against one another.
3. Tuck your chin in.

4. The snake will come and begin to nudge and climb over your body.

5. Do not panic.

6. After the snake has examined you, it will begin to swallow you from the feet end—always the feet end. Permit the snake to swallow your feet and ankles. Do not panic.

7. The snake will now begin to suck your legs into its body. You must lie perfectly still. This will take a long time.

8. When the snake has reached your knees, slowly, and with as little movement as possible, reach down, take your knife and very gently slide it into the side of the snake's mouth between the edge of its mouth and your leg. Then suddenly rip upwards, severing the snake's head.

9. Be sure you have your knife.

10. Be sure your knife is sharp.[7]

What! I'd rather do one thousand rattlesnake dances than the Brazilian Peace Corps python salsa! But it raises an appropriate point. How do you handle things when the German bombers are headed your way? How do you handle what we call the Oregon traffic jam with dozens of vehicles following a nervous farmer driving a combine on the highway? How do you handle the storms of life?

One thing I admire about Jesus the man is that He never lost His cool. Yes, He got angry. To say Jesus never got angry is to not acknowledge what the Bible says. In Mark 10:14 we read that Jesus was "indignant" when the children were prevented from coming to Him. He was angered over an injustice. And He should have been.

John 2 records Jesus' cleansing of the temple. Few would realistically argue Jesus didn't appear to be angry, but look at verse 15: "He made a scourge of cords." He stepped back, gathered materials, and strategically planned his next move. This was the action of a man under control and not a man with anger (*orgilos*) bubbling under the surface.

Each of us, like Jesus, is triggered at some point. And we all must consider how we respond and what triggered our anger. Or else, as Benjamin Franklin is believed to have said, "Whatever is begun in anger ends in shame." From experience, *orgilos* results from one of four things.

We have bitterness and resentment toward a trusted adult who wounded us. Is there someone in your past whom you have not forgiven, confronted, or spoken to a confidant about? I know men who have been dealing with woundedness their entire lives and refuse to deal with it. This will boil you inside. It reminds me of a scene in the 1984 movie *Red Dawn* when the young man whose parents were killed by Russians was carving another notch in his kill gun. The rescued fighter pilot said, "All that hate's gonna burn you up, kid."

To which he bluntly replied, "It keeps me warm."[8]

Maybe, but it will still burn you up inside.

A life event, such as war, divorce, or another tragedy, has traumatized us. Is there a traumatic event you buried in the depths of your soul, hoping it would go away? My grandfather flew a fighter plane in World War II. The pilots regularly got buzzed with a little alcohol to take the edge off before missions. How did Grandpa deal with life in the States? He became a raging alcoholic, wounded those he loved, and died way too early. Your trauma won't go away until you dig it up and deal with it.

Unconfessed and unrepented sin haunts us. I have seen men wither away and die because they refused to repent of sin. Their sin hurts not only others but also themselves. One man I know was addicted to a woman who was not his wife. Without going into detail, his entire life crumbled. It was incredibly frustrating. Exasperated by his sin, he finally shared, "I'm the most miserable man on the planet. I know what's biblical and right but refuse to stop." He had a point. He was a bitter, angry dude.

Sociopathy, narcissism, or hedonism has hardened us. Once, on a mountain bike ride, my buddy shared three things he believed led to the demise of a leader: narcissism, nepotism, and notoriety. Sociopathy and narcissism create an inability to feel empathy toward others. When a man stops caring for the things that should deeply affect him, he needs to get help before it is too late.

THE DEVIL WENT DOWN TO ...

Devil facial tumor disease is a cancer that that only affects Tasmanian devils, an animal native to Australia. The cancer spreads when one Tasmanian devil bites another around the mouth, which is a common practice among the species. The disease has ravaged Tasmania's wild devils, eradicating high-density populations. Between 1996 and 2015, the disease killed off 95 percent of some affected populations.[9]

When a man is overcome by *orgilos*, his anger will bite at the souls of those he loves. Over time he extinguishes relationships with those who venture too close. All who once loved him shy away, disappear, and only show up on major holidays.

So, keep calm and carry on.

DIAL IT IN
Small-Group Exercises

1. How are *thumos* and *orgilos* different? How can you recognize one from the other in human behavior?

2. Share about a time when you lost your cool. What kind of anger was it? Who or what was it directed to? What did you do to make it right?

3. Read James 1:19–20. How can a person express healthy anger without it leading to sin?

4. Mark 10:13–14 and John 2:13–22 contain stories where Jesus appeared to be angry, but He never sinned (Heb. 4:15). What can we learn from Jesus' anger? What things should anger us, and why?

5. In Matthew 5:21–22, Jesus taught about damning anger. Why is it so important that we deal with anger toward another?

6. How is being calm different from being patient?

7. What tools do Ephesians 4:26 and Proverbs 14:17 give to help us deal with anger in a healthy way?

ASSESSING YOUR CAPACITY

For each of the ten assessment statements, rank yourself accordingly:

(5) Strongly agree

(4) Agree

(3) Neither agree nor disagree

(2) Disagree

(1) Strongly disagree

Add up your total score at the bottom, then add the overall score in the appendix on page 277.

1. Those closest to me would say I am a great listener. _____

People never feel on edge when they are around me. _____

I do not have angry outbursts. _____

I have had the same inner circle of close friends for
    many years. _____

I do not overreact when people frustrate me. _____

I never lose my cool while driving. _____

I am known for keeping calm during a crisis. _____

When I get into a heated discussion, I look for the
    win-win. _____

I do not get offended over differing opinions. _____

I listen before I speak. _____

TOTAL SCORE _____

THE MODERATE MAN

Everything in Moderation

Many indeed with more ease practise abstinence ... than practise temperance.

—Saint Augustine

Throw moderation to the winds,
and the greatest pleasures bring the greatest pains.

—Democritus

LEGAL OR RIGHT?

Alcohol consumption is legal depending on your age. Marijuana is now legal in many locations. Before it was legal, Romans 13:1–6 had been my go-to Scripture to oppose people who argued for the value of this "natural" substance by asking, "Doesn't Proverbs 16:4 say that the Lord has made everything for its purpose?"

But a few verses down, Proverbs also says, "The highway of the upright is to depart from evil; he who watches his way preserves his life" (16:17).

A few years back, a twentysomething man approached me, "Now that marijuana is legal, like alcohol and coffee"—ouch, that hurt—"is it okay to smoke it?"

That was a loaded question, and my stance varies based on whether it has tetrahydrocannabinol (THC) and *why* a person is compelled to use it. THC is the chemical responsible for most of marijuana's psychological effects—getting stoned or high. Cannabidiol (CBD) may contain trace amounts of THC, up to 0.3 percent, and is taken for medical reasons and not to get high.

Back to the story. This man hit me below the belt with the coffee remark, so I went after a little shock and awe myself: "I've been thinking about your mom lately. She is a pretty woman. We've been texting a lot lately and decided to get a hotel room on the coast this weekend. You heard me right. I am going to have sex with *your* mom this weekend!"

Well, my shock and awe worked. He about hit the ceiling screaming, "You can't do that! You call yourself a Christian! And you're a pastor! You are married. So is my mom—to my dad, who is your friend!"

I had him right where I wanted him, so I put on the full-court press. "Did you know that even though your mom and I are both married, having sex with your mom is legal in here in Oregon? *And* it's natural, just like smoking marijuana. It must be okay, right?"

Just because something is legal and natural doesn't make it right.

He smirked, then nodded, finally understanding my analogy. I had made my point.

The bottom line is simple. Just because something is legal to consume, even if it's natural, does not make it right or good for you. Ask yourself why you want to consume it. Do you have mastery over it, or does it have mastery of you? Does it help or hinder your Christian witness? Does it compromise your mental capacity or judgment? Is it harmful to your body?

WHAT IS YOUR WHY?

The question we all must answer is, "Why do I drink alcohol, chew tobacco, smoke, overeat, or drink coffee or soda?" What is your why? The young man in my story smoked pot because he liked to get high. Biblically this is a problem.

Do you drink to get buzzed and momentarily check out? Problem.

Do you overeat because you're depressed and need comfort from food? Problem.

What is your why?

This chapter will not advocate for a specific position on the consumption of alcohol, for two reasons. First, based on one's biblical interpretation and personal history, the church is divided over the issue—an issue that I consider secondary, or probably tertiary, to the essentials of theology. As theologians have long said, "In essentials unity, in the nonessentials liberty, and above all charity." Jesus' first miracle was turning water into fine wine. Anyone would have an incredibly difficult time arguing from Scripture against alcohol consumption. Gene Getz writes, "The fact is that the Bible does not teach total abstinence—though it does teach that total abstinence might be a very important decision."[1]

Although I won't argue about whether it's okay to drink alcohol, committed believers would agree that drunkenness is a sin: "And do not get drunk with wine, for that is dissipation, but be filled with the Spirit"

(Eph. 5:18). Proverbs 20:1 also warns that "wine is a mocker, strong drink a brawler, and whoever is intoxicated by it is not wise."

I think it is also important to bring Proverbs 23:29–35 into our discussion.

> Who has woe? Who has sorrow?
> Who has contentions? Who has complaining?
> Who has wounds without cause?
> Who has redness of eyes?
> Those who linger long over wine,
> Those who go to taste mixed wine.
> Do not look on the wine when it is red,
> When it sparkles in the cup,
> When it goes down smoothly;
> At the last it bites like a serpent
> And stings like a viper.
> Your eyes will see strange things
> And your mind will utter perverse things.
> And you will be like one who lies down in the middle
>   of the sea,
> Or like one who lies down on the top of a mast.
> "They struck me, but I did not become ill;
> They beat me, but I did not know it.
> When shall I awake?
> I will seek another drink."

We should be mature enough as believers to never cause someone to stumble over the issue of alcohol because "it is good not to eat meat

or to drink wine, or to do anything by which your brother stumbles"
(Rom. 14:21). I guess I should be more sensitive to my vegan friends as
well!

Second, this chapter is not about alcohol consumption exclusively
but about *anything* we consume that harms the body, impairs the mind,
and hinders our Christian witness in any way.

Everything must be dealt with in moderation.

BESIDE WINE

When we look at the phrase "not addicted to wine"—also translated as
"not given to drunkenness" (NIV), "not be a heavy drinker" (NLT), and
"not a drunkard" (ESV), we see a word used only twice in the Bible: in
1 Timothy 3:3 and Titus 1:7. It is the Greek word *paroinos*, literally *para*
("at" or "beside") and *oinos* ("wine").

This is where it gets interesting.

Both times it's used, the word is paired with the Greek *nephalios*,
which can be translated as "sober," "watchful," "vigilant," or "temperate."
We will explain more about that word in the next chapter. Here are how
paroinos and *nephalios* are connected:

> The interesting thing is the double meaning that both
> words in this section possess. *Nēphalios* means sober,
> but it also means watchful and vigilant; *paroinos* means
> addicted to wine, but it also means quarrelsome and
> violent. The point that the Pastorals make here is that
> Christians must allow themselves no indulgence which
> would lessen their Christian vigilance or tarnish their
> Christian conduct.[2]

In other words, it isn't the substance itself that does the most damage. It's the effects, and overuse, of a particular consumed substance, whether that be coffee, processed foods (hydrogenated oils and high fructose corn syrup), tobacco (cigarettes and chewing tobacco), alcohol, or drugs (marijuana). When we lose the ability to be watchful and vigilant, whether that looks like overindulging in Thanksgiving dinner, celebrating New Year's Eve with too much alcohol, being grumpy until your morning cup of joe, or being stressed because you haven't had a bong hit, it is a problem.

Matthew Henry has this to say about *paroinos* and *nephalios*, "Sobriety and watchfulness are often in scripture put together because they mutually befriend one another."[3]

But how do you know you may have a substance issue of some kind?

ABILITY TO SAY NO

I've never abused drugs or alcohol, but potato chips are another issue. As a youth pastor, I took my youth group through the Celebrate Recovery program. Though I'm not a drug addict, the same principles apply to food, sex, and even work. It got me asking myself, *How can I tell if I have an addiction?* Let me offer a few thoughts for you to consider.

First, has anyone who cares about you ever told you that you have a problem? If so, you might have a problem. Jesus said:

> "If you abide in my word, you are truly my disciples, and you will know the truth, and the truth will set you free." They answered him, "We are offspring of Abraham and have never been enslaved to anyone. How is it that you say, 'You will become free'?"

> Jesus answered them, "Truly, truly, I say to you, every-
> one who practices sin is a slave to sin. The slave does not
> remain in the house forever; the son remains forever. So
> if the Son sets you free, you will be free indeed. I know
> that you are offspring of Abraham; yet you seek to kill
> me because my word finds no place in you. I speak of
> what I have seen with my Father, and you do what you
> have heard from your father." (John 8:31–38 ESV)

Second, are you unable to say no to the substance in question?
If those closest to you think you have a problem, it is because they have
witnessed your probable bondage. In other words, you are a slave to it.
In the context of the sexual addiction rampant among the Corinthian
Christian men of Paul's time, Paul wrote, "All things are lawful for me,
but not all things are profitable. All things are lawful for me, but I will not
be mastered by anything" (1 Cor. 6:12).

In 1998, I took high school students to Skid Row, Los Angeles, officially known as Central City East. Skid Row contains one of the largest
stable populations of people who are experiencing homelessness in the
United States (about 4,200–8,000 people). At the time it was the poor-
est place, per capita, in the United States. Its long history of police raids,
targeted city initiatives, and homelessness advocacy makes it one of the
most notable districts in Los Angeles.

The most memorable moment of that trip was one morning at a res-
taurant in Skid Row that serves huge breakfasts at insanely cheap prices
to help out people who are coming off their high or have been prostituting
all night. We gave each student ten dollars, enough to buy themselves and
a homeless person breakfast.

I bought breakfast for a guy, and Valerie, one of the girls in our youth group, bought breakfast for his girlfriend. Both the guy and his girlfriend were coming off a heroin bender. Valerie, a fifteen-year-old, blonde-haired, blue-eyed new Christian, sat wide eyed next to me as we spoke to the addicted couple. As soon as the food arrived, the girlfriend ran out the door and puked in the gutter. True story.

After I presented the gospel, the guy across from me said, "Man, I'm not interested in that Christian stuff. I don't like all that religion, rules, and stuff. I like my freedom!"

With the sounds of his girlfriend retching in the background, I asked, "How would you define this freedom you love so much?"

"Freedom?" he paused. "It's the ability to do whatever the hell I want."

"Interesting," I wondered out loud. "To me, freedom is *not* the ability to do whatever I want but the ability to say no to whatever I want." Before he could respond, I asked, "Do you have the freedom to say no to drugs?"

He started cussing wildly, grabbed his and his girlfriend's plates, and stomped out the door.

He was free to go. That was about it.

Third, have you built a tolerance to any substance? Tolerance is a pharmacological concept describing a person's reduced reaction to a drug following its repeated use. I am a 250-pound man who has no tolerance for alcohol. If I have a social drink, I must stop after one. "One and done" is my motto. Over the years I've had conversations with much smaller men who can consume four to six beers after work without any physical effects. I think these brothers either are functioning alcoholics or have built a tolerance based on chemical dependence. Either way, wouldn't you agree that they do not have freedom from alcohol?

Fourth, is your lack of moderation affecting your mind, body, or Christian witness negatively? Common afflictions like the classic beer belly, coffee headache, dad bod, munchies, and hangover are subtle signs of a life that ventured beyond moderation. Vehicular homicide, type 2 diabetes, lung cancer, and morbid obesity are more serious signs. The goal of this chapter is to help you honestly assess your life to determine whether anything has mastery over you.

Saint Augustine said it best, "Many indeed with more ease practise abstinence ... than practise temperance."[4] Sometimes it is best to stop cold turkey. I try to pray with people every chance I get. I think it is one thing I can do that a nonbeliever would never consider doing. The prayer I most often pray, and now pray over you, is James 1:5, "If any of you lacks wisdom, let him ask of God, who gives to all generously and without reproach, and it will be given to him." God *will* show you the wise way to freedom from your lack of moderation!

It is one of the few prayers that God guarantees in Scripture. God loves to gift wisdom to His children. Everything in moderation. Everything for freedom.

DIAL IT IN
Small-Group Exercises

1. Share about a time you were in bondage and what you did to break free.

2. Think about things that you take into your body, like food, coffee, sugary drinks, tobacco, alcohol, or drugs. Which ones are you most often tempted to overuse? Why?

3. What do Proverbs 20:1, Proverbs 23:29–35, and Ephesians 5:1–18 warn against?

4. Read John 8:31–38, James 5:16, and 1 John 1:9. Are you free? Confess any substances in your life you cannot say no to.

5. How do you know when you or someone you love has a problem?

6. What does 1 Corinthians 6:12 say to you?

ASSESSING YOUR CAPACITY

For each of the ten assessment statements, rank yourself accordingly:

(5) Strongly agree

(4) Agree

(3) Neither agree nor disagree

(2) Disagree

(1) Strongly disagree

Add up your total score at the bottom, then add the overall score in the appendix on page 278.

1. No food, drink, or other substance has mastery over me. _____

   I am not overweight for my age, body type, and height. _____

   I never overuse narcotics, even when I am injured. _____

   My lifestyle is not hindered because of weight-related issues. _____

   I have no addictions (phone, sports, gambling, sex, etc.). _____

   I have mastered the art of moderation with food. _____

   I am not a regular user of alcohol, tobacco, or marijuana. _____

   I am not addicted to sugar. _____

   I do not depend on caffeine to get me through the day. _____

   I have not developed a tolerance for any unhealthy substances. _____

   TOTAL SCORE _____

THE VIGILANT MAN

Keep Your Head in the Game

Conquer yourself, and you have conquered the world.

—Saint Augustine

A leader must be one who thinks clearly. He must possess the inner strength to refrain from any excess that would dull his alertness.

—John MacArthur, about the Greek word *nephalios*

SHEEP, WOLVES, AND SHEEPDOGS

While hunting in a desolate area, eight miles from the closest ranch house, I saw it. Over a mile away, the white spot stood out against an ocean of desert sage. As we approached, I saw movement—was that a tail?

Wagging.

It was a dog sitting next to a primitive doghouse and a water bowl. Watching over one thousand mindless sheep was a Great Pyrenees. I'd heard of these guardian sheepdogs but had never seen one in action. He stood resolute amid the sea of sage and sheep. The Great Pyrenees, the lone protector, can grow to 150 pounds and stand nearly three feet tall. Its weather-resistant double coat of coarse hair over a woolly undercoat makes this sheepdog resistant to the harshest weather.

From a distance, it looked like a small polar bear—except for the wagging tail of course!

In the wilderness, this breed is extremely territorial and protective of its flock or family. Its fearlessness, extreme vigilance, and fierce loyalty to duty make it an imposing guardian. This independent guardian sacrificially adapts to a nocturnal lifestyle, catching moments of sleep during daylight hours.

But here's the interesting part.

When I observed this imposing sheepdog, I couldn't spot the shepherd. Through my binoculars, I searched for the man this dog obeys, but he was nowhere to be found. Was he on lunch break? Did he make a run to the store for supplies? Was he out of view somewhere, sleeping under a tree? Where was he?

The shepherd was nowhere to be found because there was no shepherd! The Great Pyrenees lived in the wilderness alone—among the ignorant sheep keeping a vigilant eye for predators.

Alone.

Compelled by circumstance to keep its head in the game. At all costs.

Alone, protecting the weak and powerless. Alone, watching over the sheep as their only line of defense. Alone, standing in the gap. The Great Pyrenees receives no paycheck, no recognition, not even a thank-you from the clueless sheep. Its purpose is simple: to protect the sheep at all costs. Selfless, this sheepdog leads a life of solitude and sacrifice. The Great

Pyrenees is a wonderful illustration of the vigilant man who is living at his full capacity.

A sheepdog keeps its head in the game. The vigilant man does the same.

MODERATION VERSUS MINDSET

In the last chapter, "The Moderate Man," we discussed how Paul linked the words *paroinos* and *nephalios*. We addressed our relationship with consumable substances that, if overused, will inhibit the body's full function and negatively affect cognitive capacities. My deep conviction is that *nephalios* was never about substances but a mindset.

Like the Great Pyrenees, the *nephalios*, vigilant, man lives with a constant awareness of his surroundings. He fully understands the devastating consequences if he fails.

> Be of sober spirit, be on the alert. Your adversary, the
> devil, prowls around like a roaring lion, seeking some-
> one to devour. (1 Pet. 5:8)

Nephalios addresses a man's mindset, not his physical state of being. This word means properly "sober, temperate, abstinent, especially in respect to wine; then sober-minded, watchful, circumspect."[1] It is used only three times in the New Testament (1 Tim. 3:2, 11; Titus 2:2), all of which are in the Pastoral Epistles: "Older men are to be temperate, dignified, sensible, sound in faith, in love, in perseverance" (Titus 2:2).

About the *nephalios* man, Adam Clarke commented, "He must be vigilant.... Watchful; for as one who drinks is apt to sleep, so he who abstains from it is more likely to keep awake, and attend to his work and charge. A bishop has to watch over the church and watch for it; and this will require his care and circumspection."[2]

When our senses are numbed and we lose spatial awareness, we become easy prey for the hunter. In nature, a predator is easy to spot, with forward-facing eyes for laser focus, extended canines to rip and cut, smaller ears to better blend with the contours of the land, and muscular hind legs for pouncing. Prey, on the other hand, have eyes on the sides of their heads to spot predators, larger ears, olfactory receptors to see and smell an approaching predator, and generally longer legs to outrun the speed bursts of a predator.

A friend once shared about a time he was hunting deer from his rimrock vantage point. A doe was feeding beneath him, oblivious to her surroundings. The hair on his neck stood up, and he knew a predator was close. Searching through his binoculars, he spotted a mountain lion stalking the doe from the downwind side so that its scent was kept from the prey (yes, animals know about these things too). The doe was so preoccupied with eating her next meal, she didn't know she was about to become one! The lion pounced and locked its canines around the occipital bones at the base of the deer's skull, gripping tightly for another instantaneous kill.

My buddy, however, "dispatched" the lion a microsecond before the unsuspecting doe's death. I promise you, that doe went from oblivious to vigilant in a millisecond, hopefully learning a new life skill in the process! If not, it will only be a matter of time before she falls prey to another predator. Welcome to the jungle.

My buddy was able to help because, unlike the unaware deer, he had his head in the game.

BALANCING ACT

Charles Blondin was a world-famous tightrope walker. In 1859, he became the first person to walk a 1,100-foot-long and 160-foot-high tightrope across Niagara Falls. Thousands gathered around—some to heckle, some to cheer, and some to watch him meet his demise. The first time he crossed, the crowd went from being dead silent to offering thunderous applause. He then proceeded to go back and forth five more times!

He traversed the rope with no pole.

Then he took a chair halfway and sat a spell.

Then he took some juggling pins and juggled all the way across, and then he took a hot plate and made himself lunch. With every trip, the crowd got louder. For the last trip, he ratcheted up the suspense one more notch.

A wheelbarrow was unveiled. The crowd cheered, and there was no doubt in his ability to move it across. Blondin quieted the crowd and asked for a volunteer to ride in the wheelbarrow across Niagara Falls. The crowd had seen him in action, but the people didn't trust him—at least not with their lives.[3]

Like Blondin, the vigilant man masters the art of balancing life's many facets without swinging to an extreme. "*Nephalios* means 'alert,' 'watchful,' 'vigilant,' or 'clear-headed.' That may be the primary sense in this passage. A leader must be one who thinks clearly. He must possess the inner strength to refrain from any excess that would dull his alertness."[4]

The vigilant man does not swing from one side to the other like a pendulum. He is not tossed back and forth like the man James describes who "is like the surf of the sea, driven and tossed by the wind. For that man ought not to expect that he will receive anything from the Lord, being a double-minded man, unstable in all his ways" (James 1:6–8).

He doesn't live in an anxious state of tension, which is not healthy or sustainable. He refuses to act like a mental drunkard, intoxicated with opulence and gluttony. He has found the balance between being alert and relaxed—simultaneously vigilant. But this characteristic is rare among modern men who are beaten to exhaustion with jobs that demand too much time and technology that wears the sequential processing of their brain down with never-ending mind toggling—from email exchanges to text threads to social media feeds to work calls to family matters to human relationships in real time. We need to be *nephalios*—vigilant, relaxed, *and* alert—with our heads in the game, for our families and our survival.

MOVE TO YELLOW

Jeff Cooper was a Marine and World War II veteran who developed color codes of tactical alertness. He taught that more than any other weapon, the most important means of surviving a lethal confrontation is what he called "the combat mindset." As an example of this, he asked followers to watch the common house cat.

> Observe your cat. It is difficult to surprise him. Why? Naturally, his superior hearing is part of the answer, but not all of it. He moves well, using his senses fully. He is not preoccupied with irrelevancies. He's not thinking about his job or his image or his income tax. He is putting first things first, principally his physical security. Do likewise.[5]

Cooper's color codes have nothing to do with tactical situations or alertness levels but rather with one's state of mind—the combat mindset.

These codes represent the various degrees, or levels, of potential threat or danger and your suggested mindset for each.

Cooper's color codes are white, yellow, orange, and red. White is the state of being unaware and unprepared, like the sheep or the doe in the stories I shared. When I crawled into bed last night, I quickly went into white mode. Next, yellow is a relaxed but alert state of mind where you are calm but tuned in to your current environment. The orange stage is one of heightened alert. It is what happened at two in the morning yesterday when a car parked on the curb outside my house. I was asleep (white). The noise startled me awake (yellow). I got out of bed, got dressed, and moved to the window with all lights out to prevent being seen (orange). The driver got out of the car with a knife in his hand, so I ran downstairs with a baseball bat and met him at the porch (red).

Just kidding!

Actually, no one got out of the car, and it drove away minutes later. I made my way back into my bed, faded to condition white, and the rest is history.

The vigilant man lives in the yellow.

His head is always in the game even when he is relaxed. He allows nothing to compromise his mindset.

He is calm but aware and engaged with the happenings of his marriage, children, career, church, and other vital surroundings. He is stable, balanced, and alert. One of my favorite verses describes Jesus as a twelve-year-old boy: "And Jesus kept increasing in wisdom and stature, and in favor with God and men" (Luke 2:52).

Jesus was vigilant and balanced mentally ("increasing in wisdom"), physically ("stature"), spiritually ("favor with God"), and socially ("favor ... with men"). The vigilant man must balance his life in all areas.

This is a massive challenge for compartmentalized men like us. For example, if a man masters vigilance with his work but fails to do so with his wife, his marriage struggles. If a man is vigilant with his marriage but neglects his children, those relationships will suffer for it.

STANDING OVERWATCH

In July our blueberry bushes produce more berries than I can pick. My granddaughter and the neighborhood kids love to invade the shrubs with their hands going from the berry bush to their mouths nonstop. Even passersby, unaware of my presence, swipe a few off the bushes.

Why?

It's low-hanging fruit. Close to the path. Perfect for children.

Where should the dialed in man maintain vigilance? Let's look at five areas of low-hanging fruit for the vigilant man.

Your big picture. I spend my predawn hours reading my Bible and good books, praying, and thinking about God, life, and those I love. My wife knows this time is sacred. Without it, I operate at less than full capacity. Like the sheepdog, you should find a good spot where you can habitually reflect on the panoramic view of your life.

Your mental state. How full is your emotional tank? What are you learning? What is God saying? Is your mind rested, alert, and ready? This morning I ran into a business owner at a local coffee shop. It was early. I needed to sit and think about this chapter from different vantage points. He shared that he goes there most mornings to grab some coffee, get alone, and go on a prayer walk to get things in order. This is a best-kept secret for dialed in men. Why they don't share it with more people is beyond me. Maybe it is too sacred to share. Maybe it has become such a ritual that it seems mundane. Maybe they simply assume it is what everyone does.

But everyone does not. Take time each day to think, reflect, and listen to God's whisper.

Your physical well-being. I used to brag about how little sleep I needed to function. I thought it was a badge of honor. What an idiot! Don't be like that. God made us to sleep one-third of our lives and take one full day off each week to rest, recover, and relish the ones we love. Anything less than that will lower your vigilance capacity.

Women are much better at listening to their bodies than us guys, but as I get older, I'm listening more to my body. Is it tired from sleep deprivation? Is it irritable from work exhaustion? Is it sore from muscle exertion? Is it inflamed from poor food consumption? Is it hungry from starvation?

Your spiritual commitment to God. Am I loving God at full capacity, or is sin hindering me in some way? Am I hungry to pursue God? Am I involved in a local church, and does the leadership know my name? Do I love the Lord more than I did yesterday? Am I walking in biblical obedience? Am I reading the Word daily? Am I giving a minimum of 10 percent to kingdom causes I care about? How is my prayer life? Do those who know me best see my growing faith? How is my local church doing?

Your social relationships. How is my marriage? Am I deeply connected to my wife? Do we make love often? Do I still pursue her? Are my children healthy, respectful, and obedient? Are my relationships healthy? Do I need to make amends with anyone? Are my spiritual leaders healthy? Do any of my buddies have blind spots I need to talk to them about? Who can I invite over for a meal? How can I pray for my political leaders? What is the state of my local, state, and federal government?

Keep your head in the game.

DIAL IT IN
Small-Group Exercises

1. What are some distinctions between being moderate (*paroinos*) in chapter 6 and being vigilant (*nephalios*)?

2. Sheep, wolf, or sheepdog—which best describes you, and why?

3. Look at John 10:10, 1 Corinthians 16:13, and 1 Peter 5:8. What insights about vigilance do you gather from these passages?

4. Look at the three times *nephalios* is used in the Bible (1 Timothy 3:2, 11; Titus 2:2). What insights do you have?

5. Assess your vigilance based on Luke 2:52. Where can you grow?

6. Take a moment to review some of the questions asked in the "Standing Overwatch" section of this chapter. Where can you grow? Where are you strong?

7. Pick one question from each category to ask another man. If you are reading this solo, have your wife ask you one from each category.

ASSESSING YOUR CAPACITY

For each of the ten assessment statements, rank yourself accordingly:

(5) Strongly agree

(4) Agree

(3) Neither agree nor disagree

(2) Disagree

(1) Strongly disagree

Add up your total score at the bottom, then add the overall score in the appendix on page XX.

1. I rarely overcommit myself.   _____

I regularly make time to regroup, reflect, and refresh.   _____

I use all my allotted vacation days.   _____

I am emotionally stable and under control in every
situation I face.   _____

I am aware of my surroundings and am rarely caught
off guard.   _____

I seek to find the truth between two extremes.   _____

When faced with unforeseen events, I respond in a
sober and controlled manner.   _____

I adjust quickly to challenging obstacles.   _____

I appreciate the statement "This too shall pass."   _____

I never use "I was too busy" as an excuse for not
fulfilling a commitment.   _____

TOTAL SCORE   _____

7

THE PEACEMAKER

Peacefaker, Peacebreaker, or Peacemaker?

Now the overseer is ... not quarrelsome.

—1 Timothy 3:2–3 (NIV)

Peacemakers see conflict as an opportunity to solve problems in a way that not only benefits everyone involved but also honors God. They use conflict to glorify God, serve others, and become more like Christ.

—Ken Sande and Kevin Johnson, *Resolving Everyday Conflict*

THE PEACEMAKER

In 1847, Samuel Colt accepted an order for one thousand revolvers from Captain Samuel Walker of the Texas Rangers.[1] Before Colt began mass-producing his revolvers, handguns had not played a significant role in the history of the American West. Short-barreled handguns were costly and inaccurate. At the time, the sidearm of choice was the bowie knife.

In 1873, Colt's Manufacturing Company produced a revolver called the Colt Single Action Army, which became famously known in American history as the "Peacemaker."[2]

It's a single-action handgun with a revolving cylinder holding six cartridges that has been offered in over thirty different calibers and various barrel lengths. Because of the impact of Colt's repeating weapon design, a popular saying during that time was "God made men and Sam Colt made them equal."[3]

There is a reason the revolver was nicknamed the Peacemaker, not the Peacekeeper. Those concepts oppose each other. In this chapter, you will learn about the peacemaker and how he is different from the peacekeeper (a.k.a. peacefaker[4]) and peacebreaker.

The Greek word translated only in 1 Timothy 3:3 and Titus 3:2 as "peaceable," or "not quarrelsome" (NIV), is *amachon*. This word *does not* describe someone who is seeking a physical altercation but refers to a person who is seeking a verbal confrontation. The root word is *mache,* meaning "fight or combat." Thus, the literal translation of *amachon* means "not a fighter."[5]

The peacemaker opposes the person whom some translations call "quarrelsome" (NIV), "brawler" (KJV), "addicted to contention" (Darby), and "contentious" (ASV). Contentious people love to argue, disrupt, and be contrary. They pride themselves in being the "devil's advocate." They annoy with their words. They love to debate, even if they don't believe in the stance they take. They get off on stirring the pot.

The quarrelsome individual loves to debate everything, even if he doesn't care about the topic or believe he is right. I call this person a contrarian because he finds a sick sense of pleasure in arguing with others. He enjoys using his rebuttal skills to twist words and create confusion. His end game is to get adverse reactions from people whom he knows offer no physical threat.

The real question for the quarrelsome person is, Why? What is your motivation? Is your heart pure, or are you leveraging your knowledge over someone else? Is it your desire to relate the truth or to test those who may not possess your debating skills? Do you simply want to argue, or are you truly seeking to understand? Doesn't the Bible say, "Knowledge puffs up while love builds up" (1 Cor. 8:1 NIV)?

THE BLESSED PEACEMAKER

I've spent substantial space explaining the negative characteristics of the contentious or argumentative person. But what was Paul after? What's the goal? What positive trait does the dialed in man carry in his twenty-round magazine of masculine qualities?

One word.

Peacekeeper.

During Jesus' famous Sermon on the Mount, He listed many things His followers could do to be blessed. In Matthew 5:9 we see one of those: "Blessed are the peacemakers, for they shall be called sons of God."

Notice what Jesus didn't say. He didn't say *peacekeepers* but rather *peacemakers*.

I hold that these words oppose each other. Diametrically. We are blessed when we are unified. God's desire is unity. In the High Priestly Prayer, Jesus prayed for unity specifically:

> The glory which You have given Me I have given to them,
> that they may be one, just as We are one; I in them and
> You in Me, that they may be perfected in unity, so that

the world may know that You sent Me, and loved them,

even as You have loved Me. (John 17:22–23)

On the last night with His disciples, Jesus said, "A new command-ment I give to you, that you love one another, even as I have loved you, that you also love one another. By **this** all men will know that you are My disciples, if you have love for one another" (John 13:34–35).

You cannot love without unity. It is not possible.

Later, Paul reminded the church at Ephesus, "Therefore I, the pris-oner of the Lord, implore you to walk in a manner worthy of the calling with which you have been called, with all humility and gentleness, with patience, showing tolerance for one another in love, being diligent to pre-serve the unity of the Spirit in the bond of peace" (Eph. 4:1–3).

In Psalm 133:1 we read, "Behold, how good and how pleasant it is for brothers to dwell together in unity!"

Mike Huckabee had some wise words regarding peace: "Jesus said, 'Blessed are the peacemakers.' And I think a lot of people don't under-stand that there's a difference between a peace lover and a peacemaker. Everybody loves peace but wearing jewelry around your neck and saying, 'I love peace' doesn't bring it."[6]

God is uninterested in peacekeepers or peace lovers. He is looking to bless the peacemakers. Do you want to be blessed? Become a peacemaker. Let's unpack the three ways people deal with relational tension and con-flict when they arise.

PEACEFAKER (A.K.A. PEACEKEEPER)

From 2012 to 2017, I was blessed to travel to San Pedro, Belize, over a dozen times, most of those as the Discipleship Training School speaker at the Youth with a Mission (YWAM) base, which sadly closed a few years back. Between the people, food, and opportunities along the 190-mile Belize Barrier Reef, Ambergris Caye has become one of my favorite places on the planet.

Shanna and I loved renting a golf cart and driving on Front Street, Middle Street, and Back Street in San Pedro on its warm Caribbean nights. One of my fondest memories from our golf cart dates is when I accidentally turned the wrong way on a one-way street (there are only three streets in San Pedro), almost hitting a frantic police officer who screamed, "Turn around now before someone gives you a ticket!"

Someone? Uh, aren't you the police? Aren't you that someone?

We laughed, put the cart in reverse, and got out of there before "someone" wrote us up!

Mr. Policeman wasn't willing to accept the responsibility entrusted to him by the local government. In doing so, this man who was hired as a peacemaker became a peacekeeper (a.k.a. peacefaker). For whatever reason—fear, laziness, or apathy—our police friend chose to turn his back on his responsibility instead of facing it. In this case, we were thankful for it! But as believers, we must take responsibility for maintaining healthy relationships. Sometimes we take Scripture out of context to avoid doing what is right even if it's difficult.

For example, Proverbs 20:3 says, "Avoiding a fight is a mark of honor; only fools insist on quarreling" (NLT). Taking this solo verse as an absolute rule for every situation would undermine much of what Jesus taught and accomplished in His ministry. Remember that He said, "Do not think that I came to bring peace on the earth; I did not come to bring peace, but a sword" (Matt. 10:34).

In their excellent book *Resolving Everyday Conflict*, Ken Sande and Kevin Johnson wrote, "There are three basic ways people respond to conflict. We choose to escape, attack, or make peace.... Using an escape response usually means I'm intent on peacefaking, trying to make things look good even when they aren't."[7] The peacefaker escapes, evades, and excuses away conflict to keep the peace but fails to understand how different this is from making peace. They escape by running away or living in denial.

According to Sande and Johnson, all peacefaking responses have one thing in common: the focus is usually on me.[8]

There was a season when I lost the respect of a handful of men who were once friends. I won't share details except to say that, like the San Pedro policeman, I failed in peacemaking, acted cowardly, and I am still paying the price over ten years later. I turned a blind eye to a problem instead of dealing with it like a man. Then I overcorrected, swung to the opposite end of the pendulum, and went into full-attack mode. It wasn't until the damage had been done that I sought forgiveness. Sadly, it was too late. I'm writing this section out of failure but determined to be a peacemaker and reject cowardice.

Here is the kicker. At the time I justified both peacefaking *and* peacebreaking responses as right *and* biblical! It is a slippery slope when we go into self-preservation mode and justify sin instead of objectively diving into the Word of God.

PEACEBREAKER

Unlike the peacefaker who runs from a conflict, the peacebreaker attacks with actions or words. Attacking can take the form of litigation, which is interesting since we are living in the most litigated time in world history. Or peacebreaking can escalate to full-blown assault. We see it every day.

A heinous example of peacebreaking is an event that received international media coverage in 1993 when, after claims of years of rape and abuse, Lorena Bobbitt cut off her husband's penis while he was asleep, drove away with it in her hand, but ultimately threw the severed appendage out the window because of the difficulty driving with one hand! Fortunately, she called 911 and told them what happened and where to find the penis. After an exhaustive search, it was found and reattached after a lengthy surgery.

When I go into peacebreaking mode, the focus of my attack turns to you. Some call this gaslighting. Others call it finger-pointing. Either way, it is a full-blown attack against the other person. The other person is to blame. They are at fault. And you will make sure they pay. When I care more about winning than my relationship with someone, I become a peacebreaker.[9]

PEACEMAKER

With just over three thousand residents, the Hawaiian island of Lanai has a saying, "What happens on Lanai—everyone knows." Because of the generosity of some friends, it has become a regular vacation stop for us, for which we are deeply grateful. Our friends recently purchased a side-by-side (a gas-powered golf cart) that was used only off the road. The day before leaving, I drove a quarter mile on the main road to the only gas station on the island. I was promptly pulled over by a police officer, who must have called for backup because I was quickly surrounded by every police vehicle on the island, along with a bunch of curious locals.

"What happens on Lanai ..."

I was told that the golf cart was a "gold mine of infractions" and enthusiastically handed a citation. The policeman was kind enough, once he deduced that our violation was made from a place of ignorance, not to haul us to jail. He informed us that if I called a certain number and went to online court, it would most likely be thrown out.

I did. And it was.

He was a true peacemaker.

In *The Purpose Driven Life*, Rick Warren said, "Peacemaking is not **avoiding conflict**. Running from a problem, pretending it doesn't exist, or being afraid to talk about it is actually cowardice.... Always giving in, acting like a doormat, and allowing others to always run over you is not what Jesus had in mind."[10]

Ignoring my questionable golf cart navigational skills, we can see how the similar situations in San Pedro and Lanai rendered such different responses. What I've learned through failure, success, and the example of others is that sometimes you must disrupt the peace to make peace. Sometimes you must stir the pot to make the stew. Sande and Johnson write that peacemakers "seize every chance to strengthen relationships, preserve valuable resources, and make their lives clear evidence of the love and power of Christ."[11]

Conflict is a part of life. Unless you move to a remote place, stay in a cave, and live off the land, you will experience conflict. This is because relationships involve people, people are broken, and broken people create conflict.

The peacefaker is usually focused on me.

The peacebreaker is zeroed in on the other person.

The peacemaker is fixated on Christ and how to glorify Him during the conflict.

Sande and Johnson's book, *Resolving Everyday Conflict*, is short and wonderful. I highly recommend Ken Sande's Peacemaker Ministries and its excellent tools for conflict resolution and peacemaking. *Resolving Everyday Conflict* includes excellent suggestions for the peacemaker, which the authors call the Four Gs.

Go higher. How can I focus on God and what the Bible teaches in this situation? When emotions are hot, it is wise to ask a trusted friend about their interpretation of Scripture regarding conflict resolution.

Get real. What is my part in this conflict? Where can I take responsibility? What role did I play in the current situation? How did I contribute to where we are now?

Gently engage. How can I help others see the error of their ways? How can I help others accept responsibility for their actions? How can I gently engage in the tough conversation about sin?

Get together. How can I give forgiveness and help those involved reach a peaceful solution? Who needs to help mediate this conflict? What nonthreatening environment can help achieve a win-win for all parties?[12]

DIAL IT IN
Small-Group Exercises

1. Consider 1 Timothy 3:2–3 and Titus 3:1–2 in several different Bible translations. How else could you translate the word for "peaceable"?

2. What suggestions did Jesus teach about peacekeeping in Matthew 6:12–15, Matthew 18:15–20, and Luke 6:27–36?

3. What is the difference between the peacefaker, peacebreaker, and peacemaker? Which of these do you most often default to and why?

4. What else do Romans 12:17–19 and Titus 3:10–11 teach about how to make peace and when it is time to change tactics?

5. What do Galatians 6:1–5 and Ephesians 4:1–3 teach us about peacemaking? Share about a time this was used on you.

6. Discuss this quote from Dietrich Bonhoeffer: "Nothing can be more cruel than the tenderness that consigns another to his sin. Nothing can be more compassionate than the severe rebuke that calls a brother back from the path of sin."[13]

7. Review the Four Gs of peacemaking. Do any of the four stand out?

8. Is there a situation you need to step into as a peacemaker?

ASSESSING YOUR CAPACITY

For each of the ten assessment statements, rank yourself accordingly:

(5) Strongly agree

(4) Agree

(3) Neither agree nor disagree

(2) Disagree

(1) Strongly disagree

Add up your total score at the bottom, then add the overall score in the appendix on page 279.

1. People tell me that I am a team player who works well with others. _____

When I have a problem with someone, I go to them instead of ignoring it. _____

I do not believe competition should lead to division. _____

I never purposely back people into a corner with my interrogations. _____

I get annoyed with people who love to argue. _____

I believe time does not solve all problems or heal all wounds. _____

It is better to speak up than to stay silent. _____

I believe that evil triumphs when good men do nothing. _____

I am known as a man who takes an active interest in others. _____

I am known as a peacemaker. _____

TOTAL SCORE _____

THE PROTECTOR

Never Start a Fight—Finish It

There is one fairly good reason for fighting—and that is, if the other man starts it.... When you can be perfectly certain that the other man started them, then is the time when you might have a sort of duty to stop him.

—T. H. White, *The Once and Future King*

Though God hates bullying, too many Christians don't.

—Paul Coughlin, *Free Us from Bullying*

SUNDAY SCHOOL SUPERINTENDENT

Our organization, Men in the Arena, is named after a speech given by Theodore Roosevelt entitled "Citizenship in a Republic." Roosevelt had a deep and real faith, read his Bible regularly, regularly attended church, and publicly encouraged church attendance. When gas rationing was introduced during the First World War, he walked three miles from his home to the local church and back, even after a serious operation had made it difficult for him to travel by foot.

He didn't allow any engagement to keep him from going to church, and he remained a fervent advocate of the Bible throughout his adult life. According to Christian Reisner, "Religion was as natural to Mr. Roosevelt as breathing."[1]

But Sunday school was not.

A negative experience as a young man attending Harvard University got him fired from teaching Sunday school. One Sunday, one of his students came to class with a black eye and confessed that he had been fighting. Fighting on Sunday before church! The boy explained that a bigger, older bully had been pinching his sister, so he stood up for her and ended up with a black eye. Roosevelt told the boy that he had done the right thing and gave him a dollar. Hearing about this Sunday school exchange, the superintendent relieved the future United States president of his Sunday school teaching duties. Roosevelt never taught Sunday school again.[2]

But he knew something many do not. Never start a fight. Finish it.

DO SOMETHING WHILE I PRAY AND WATCH

What would you have done if you were the Sunday school superintendent? If we are honest, many of our churches would have rebuked the teacher, sent a church-wide email, and compelled him to apologize to the child and his parents for such false teaching.

And we wonder why churches have a hard time finding men to teach Sunday school.

What should the boy have done? Allow his little sister to get hurt by a bully? Pray and ask God to be merciful while passively watching? Run to find an adult to break it up? Turn the other cheek? The title of this chapter implies what any man should do. Only a coward would excuse failing to protect the weak from a bully. The church has taken one passage of Jesus' teachings grossly out of context and somehow left the entirety of the Bible out in the process.

What do you think Jesus would have done in the same situation? Do you think Jesus would have physically intervened if He saw a child being violated? Remember, this is our Savior who said, "If anyone causes one of these little ones—those who believe in me—to stumble, it would be better for them to have a large millstone hung around their neck and to be drowned in the depths of the sea" (Matt. 18:6 NIV).

Was God joking when He said, "Defend the weak and the fatherless; uphold the cause of the poor and the oppressed. Rescue the weak and the needy; deliver them from the hand of the wicked" (Ps. 82:3–4 NIV)? I hear you justifying cowardice: "Yeah, but that was the Old Testament. The New Testament tells us to turn the other cheek."

But does it?

Times have changed. Yes. But did God change? Isn't "Jesus Christ ... the same yesterday and today and forever" (Heb. 13:8)?

I think Jesus would agree that His followers should never start a fight. Instead, they should be ready to finish it. There are those rare times when the only way to intervene on behalf of the powerless is to get physical, but *most of the time*, finishing a fight means speaking out and acting on behalf of the weak and defenseless, those without an advocate. When we look at the entirety of the Bible and the history of the world since then, what do we see?

THE STRIKER

Let's look at the original Greek used only in 1 Timothy 3:3 and in this quote from Titus 1:7 (NIV): "Since an overseer manages God's household, he must [not] be ... violent." Staying true to our theme of using a positive word to describe each of our twenty qualities, I chose the word *protector* because the protector stands in opposition to the bully, or "striker" as described in some translations.

When I think of the "striker," I go back to a garage full of dudes on April 15, 2005, and my introduction to the Ultimate Fighting Championship (UFC 52). The main event was the historic third bout between light heavyweight champ Randy Couture and Chuck Liddell. Liddell knocked Couture out in the first round, stealing the light heavyweight title and defeating Couture for the second time, solidifying him as one of the greatest strikers in UFC history.

I left the garage that night a new mixed martial arts fan drenched in sweat.

The Greek word *plektes*, mentioned only twice in the New Testament, is translated as "pugnacious," "violent" (NIV), and "striker" (KJV). The striker uses verbal and physical aggression on weaker individuals. He is a bully. His nefarious intent is to inflict his will upon another person.

Paul Coughlin defines bullying as "repeated.... victimization without provocation."[3]

Comparing the protector with the bully, Benjamin Disraeli is believed to have said, "Courage is fire, and bullying is smoke."

One of my favorite classics about King Arthur and the Knights of the Round Table is *The Once and Future King*. Author T. H. White used a common theme throughout the book: Might does not make right! Right makes right! Our fallen world is saturated with fatherlessness, oppression, brokenness, and poverty. There are unlimited causes to stand for and people to protect and defend. Pray and ask God to wreck you for the things that wreck Him.

Studying *plektes*—"striker," or "one who is violent or pugnacious"— carefully, I've concluded that Paul was saying not to be the bully but the man who protects and defends against the bully. The protector is the greatest adversary and threat to the bully because he dares to stand up and call him out for who he truly is—a gutless coward.

A NEW KIND OF BULLY

My crusade against bullies started at an early age when my dad warned me never to start a fight. I vividly remember Dad telling me, his four-year-old son, "Never start a fight. But if anyone ever threatens your brother or sister, you'd better finish it."

When we consider what Paul was saying about the striker, we must look at the context in which Paul was writing. There was no technology beyond candlelight. If you wanted to say something, it had to be face-to-face. If you wanted to bully someone, you had to look them in the eye.

Not today.

With digital technology, it is easier than ever to be a bully—a cyberbully. It is a great time in history to be a coward, hiding behind a computer screen, striking with vulgarities through a keyboard. But the identity of a bully—whether it be an abusive boss, pulpit bully, violent school kid, or snotty middle school girl—someone who victimizes others without provocation.

My friend Paul Coughlin's anti-bullying organization, the Protectors, encourages passive witnesses of bullying to courageously act to protect others.

Let me say this loud and clear. I'm not a fan of violence. I haven't thrown a punch since elementary school and, God willing, do not intend to. We should do everything within our power to avoid physical altercations. Protecting the weak and powerless against the bully usually does not require a physical altercation. But it might.

I believe King Solomon was under the inspiration of the Holy Spirit when he penned the words, "There is an appointed time for everything. And there is a time for every event under heaven…. A time to tear apart and a time to sew together; a time to be silent and a time to speak. A time to love and a time to hate; a time for war and a time for peace" (Eccl. 3:1, 7–8).

Physical force should only be implemented when you witness someone being violated *and* there is no other reasonable option left. Most of the time we fight with our time, talents, resources, and prayer.

But there may be a time when a helpless person is being manhandled by a bully, and when that time comes, your response should be swift, aggressive, absolute, and violent if necessary.

Never start a fight. Finish it.

CHEEK TURNING

Sitting Bull is famously known for leading the confederated Lakota people against the United States invasion of their native lands. He is most remembered as the man who decimated Colonel George Custard's Seventh Cavalry on June 25, 1876 at the Battle of the Little Bighorn. Whatever you might think about Sitting Bull, here's an on-target explanation he expressed about a man's role in protecting the weak against a bully:

Warriors are not what you think of as warriors. The warrior is not someone who fights, because no one has the right to take another life. The warrior, for us, is one who sacrifices himself for the good of others. His task is to take care of the elderly, the defenseless, those who cannot provide for themselves, and above all, the children, the future of humanity.[4]

I know what you've been thinking all along. Both times Paul used the word *plektes*—striker—it is used as something not to do. Why then do I seem to be advocating use of force when Jesus taught His followers to turn the other cheek?

You have heard that it was said, "An eye for an eye, and a tooth for a tooth." But I say to **you**, do not resist an evil person; but whoever slaps **you** on **your** right cheek, turn the other to him also. If anyone wants to sue **you** and take **your** shirt, let him have **your** coat also. Whoever forces **you** to go one mile, go with him two. Give to him who asks of **you**, and do not turn away from him who wants to borrow from **you**. (Matt. 5:38–42)

I believe historically this passage has been taken out of context by well-intentioned Bible teachers. John MacArthur wrote, "Probably no part of the Sermon on the Mount has been so misinterpreted and misapplied as 5:38–42. It has been interpreted to mean that Christians are to be sanctimonious doormats. It has been used to promote pacifism, conscientious objection to military service, lawlessness, anarchy, and a host of other positions that it does not support."[5]

In Matthew 10:34 Jesus said, "Do not think that I came to bring peace on the earth; I did not come to bring peace, but a sword." Then in Luke 22:35–38, He said,

> "When I sent you out without money belt and bag and sandals, you did not lack anything, did you?" They said, "No, nothing." And He said to them, "But now, whoever has a money belt is to take it along, likewise also a bag, and whoever has no sword is to sell his coat and buy one. For I tell you that this which is written must be fulfilled in Me, 'And He was numbered with transgressors'; for that which refers to Me has its fulfillment." They said, "Lord, look, here are two swords." And He said to them, "It is enough."

So, what did Jesus mean when He told His followers to "turn the other cheek"? In Matthew 5:38–42, Jesus used the personal pronoun *you* or *your* nine times.

In 2 Timothy 3:12 Paul gave a wonderful promise that "indeed, all who desire to live godly in Christ Jesus will be persecuted."

Not to be outdone, Peter wrote, "For what credit is there if, when you sin and are harshly treated, you endure it with patience? But if when you do what is right and suffer for it you patiently endure it, this finds favor with God" (1 Pet. 2:20–21).

Persecution for faith in Jesus was not only expected but desired among historic believers. Tertullian was the early Christian theologian often paraphrased as saying, "The blood of the martyrs is the seed of the church."

Jesus' followers should welcome and willingly allow persecution for their faith in Jesus, just as Jesus accepted persecution for His message. When persecution comes our way, we should turn the other cheek. Because Christian persecution is highly esteemed, believers should not defend themselves against it but trust that we will be strong enough to endure it and glorify Him in the end.

But there are two times when we should not tolerate such aggression.

WHEN TO FIGHT

First, when someone attempts to violate me for reasons *other than* my faith in Jesus, I have a biblical mandate to steward my body as God's temple (1 Cor. 6:19–20) and preserve my life for the glory of God. Just as I would ward off a hungry bear, I should also defend myself against the figurative wolves that attempt to rob my dignity. It's like the story of the atheist who fought against a bear attack but was badly mauled and about to be eaten. In a final effort to save his life, he prayed, "God, I don't believe in You. Never have. But if You exist, I want You to turn this bear into a Christian before he eats me."

No sooner had he prayed this than the bear suddenly dropped him from its mouth, bowed its head, and prayed, "Dear Lord, thank You for this delicious man I'm about to devour! Amen."

I love it!

Second, as a passionate believer in the sanctity of life, I will protect life—including mine—at all costs. In other words, I believe Jesus taught His followers to turn the other cheek when we are persecuted for our faith. In Matthew 5:38–42, Jesus strategically focused on the individual being attacked and never commented about what to do when we witness others slapped by the predatory bully.

Why?

Why did He leave others out of the "turn the other cheek" discourse? Because the requirement to protect the defenseless was common knowledge to ancient listeners, who knew that anything less was a sin. Jewish people viewed defending the weak and powerless as a mandate from Yahweh, and Jesus knew that it did not need to be mentioned. It was a deep-seated assumption of their culture: "Learn to do good; seek justice, reprove the ruthless, defend the orphan, plead for the widow" (Isa. 1:17).

To ignore those being systematically violated is a sin. The Jewish people believed with conviction that their role as a nation was to "open your mouth for the mute, for the rights of all the unfortunate. Open your mouth, judge righteously, and defend the rights of the afflicted and needy" (Prov. 31:8–9).

In other words, never start a fight. Finish it instead.

DIAL IT IN
Small-Group Exercises

1. Review 1 Timothy 3:2–3 and Titus 1:7 using various Bible translations. How do you interpret the Greek word *plektes*?

2. Compare Paul Coughlin's statement "Though God hates bullying, too many Christians don't"[6] with the saying "The only thing necessary for the triumph of evil is that good men do nothing."

3. How do you interpret Matthew 5:38–42 against the whole of the Bible and, specifically, Matthew 10:34 and Luke 22:35–38?

4. What is the Christian response to Matthew 10:22, 2 Timothy 3:12, and 1 Peter 2:20–21?

5. How can a protector use force without using violence? What are nonviolent ways to fight for the people groups you care deeply about? Consider Proverbs 31:8–9 (NLT).

6. What are you currently fighting for through the stewardship of your time, talents, and resources? Who needs your protection right now?

ASSESSING YOUR CAPACITY

For each of the ten assessment statements, rank yourself accordingly:

(5) Strongly agree

(4) Agree

(3) Neither agree nor disagree

(2) Disagree

(1) Strongly disagree

Add up your total score at the bottom, then add the overall score in the appendix on page 280.

1. I try to make peace when a conflict begins, rather than welcoming a fight. _____

People do not consider me to be argumentative. _____

There is no reason to fight except to defend oneself or to protect the powerless. _____

I have never touched a loved one in anger. _____

I never speak to others in a harsh and abrasive manner. _____

I have never thrown or punched anything in anger. _____

I never gossip about people behind their backs. _____

People are not threatened by me. _____

I do not pummel people who disagree with me on social media. _____

I refuse to engage in fights over politics. _____

TOTAL SCORE _____

THE HOSPITABLE MAN

Mi Casa Es Su Casa

If a man be gracious and courteous to strangers,
it shows he is a citizen of the world.

—Francis Bacon

When you open your home to strangers,
you are opening your home to the Lord Jesus.

—Ray Pritchard, *Man of Honor*

LONE SURVIVOR

The book *Lone Survivor* is Marcus Luttrell's account of Operation Red
Wings, an unsuccessful 2005 counterinsurgent mission in northeastern
Afghanistan, during which a four-man SEAL team was given the task of
tracking down the Taliban leader Ahmad Shah. A movie with the same
title was produced in 2013.

Three of the four team members were killed after being discovered by local herdsmen and subsequently ambushed. Luttrell, the lone survivor, was left unconscious with several fractures, a broken back, and numerous shrapnel wounds. He was ultimately rescued after local Pashtun villagers, one of them being Mohammad Gulab, protected him against a Taliban-linked militia. Why? The Pashtun people live according to an ancient and fiercely independent tradition called Pashtunwali.

Thirteen principles form the major components of Pashtunwali. Two of their principles saved Luttrell's life and led the Pashtun people to ferociously protect it for days with no regard for themselves:

> **Hospitality** (*melmastyā'*)–Showing hospitality and profound respect to all visitors, regardless of race, religion, national affiliation or economic status and doing so without any hope of remuneration or favor.
>
> **Asylum** (*nənawā'te*)–People are protected at all costs; even those running from the law must be given refuge until the situation can be clarified.[1]

HORSESHOES AND WAGON TRAINS

Melmastyā' and *nənawā'te* are virtues practiced by the Pashtun people, even if it means risking their lives. Dating back more than a thousand years before Christ or the founding of the Islamic religion, these traditions embody hospitality and give us a great starting point to deconstruct our modern view of the world. Unfortunately, the Western understanding of hospitality is, quite frankly, not biblical. I confess that my understanding of hospitality was errant until I dove headlong into its meaning and power for ancient believers. Hospitality was a tool God used to build the fledgling church a few years after Christ's ascension. First, let's look at what hospitality is not.

Hospitality is not a spiritual gift. Have you heard someone say, "I would invite people over more often, but hospitality isn't my gift"? Hospitality is a means through which spiritual gifts such as mercy, serving, giving, and evangelizing are displayed.

The problem is that many popular spiritual gifts tests include hospitality as a gift, citing 1 Peter 4:8–10 as a reference: "Above all, keep fervent in your love for one another, because love covers a multitude of sins. Be **hospitable to one another** without complaint. As each one has received a special gift, employ it in serving one another as good stewards of the manifold grace of God."

Peter admonished *everyone* to show hospitality, not just those who have a natural propensity toward hospitality. After making this point, he added that we should also use any unique, or "special," gifts to serve one another.

Hospitality is not mentioned in any of the three primary sections dedicated to spiritual gifts: Romans 12:3–8, 1 Corinthians 12:1–31, and 1 Corinthians 14:1–19. Like Peter, after offering a brief teaching on spiritual gifts, Paul encouraged all believers to do certain things:

> Love must be sincere. Hate what is evil; cling to what is good. Be devoted to one another in love. Honor one another above yourselves. Never be lacking in zeal, but keep your spiritual fervor, serving the Lord. Be joyful in hope, patient in affliction, faithful in prayer. Share with the Lord's people who are in need. **Practice hospitality.** (Rom. 12:9–13 NIV)

Even the most casual reading makes it clear that hospitality is not a spiritual gift but a Christian virtue for all believers.

Hospitality is not entertaining people you know. Ray Pritchard explains our misunderstanding of hospitality this way: "Unfortunately, we think hospitality is what happens when we get dressed up and invite our friends over for a party. That's nice, and it's good, but it's not hospitality."[2] Hospitality has little to do with inviting our friends over, creating a welcoming environment for our children's friends, or hosting church events in our home. You may want to reread that. Opening your home to people you already know is an incorrect interpretation of biblical hospitality. Aren't you glad we got that straightened out?

If Mohammad Gulab of the Pashtun people had spoken Spanish, he would have told Marcus Luttrell, "Mi casa es su casa."

Hospitality is not a place. I confess that I am guilty of something on Sundays at the church I attend. I'm working on it and think I'm improving. I call it "circling the wagons." My favorite part about Sunday is fellowship with the guys I haven't seen all week. I look forward to before and after church—the actual service is a bonus.

On Sundays, my buddies and I look strangely similar to a pioneer wagon train formed into a circle to keep dangerous intruders out. Whenever we do this, we are telling guests and other guys who aren't in our wagon perimeters, "You aren't welcome here."

Instead, we should break the circle into horseshoes that invite people in. Hospitality is not a place. It is an attitude that says, "Mi casa es su casa."

We live in a world that warns its children of "stranger danger." Parents should use wisdom regarding strangers, but when we teach our children that strangers are dangerous and must be avoided at all costs, we run the risk of steering our kids toward becoming adults who, rather than following the example of Jesus, avoid people who are different from them.

We are all strangers to someone. I thank God for the two strange young men who fixed our golf cart when it stopped running in the middle of San Pedro, Belize, one night at ten o'clock. I thank God for the strange man who jumped Shanna's car battery in the employee parking lot at one in the morning after a late-night flight. I'm thankful for the strange young man who gave me water and rode with me after I bonked halfway into Moab's Slickrock Bike Trail. I'm thankful for the stranger who took care of Shanna and me in Isla Mujeres, Mexico, when we needed direction.

ESTÁ EN SU CASA

Like the Pashtun people, the early church highly valued hospitality. In the days of the great Roman persecutions by Emperors Nero, Marcus Aurelius, Decius, Trebonianus Gallus, and Valerian, Christians were banished, persecuted, and rendered homeless.

Christians traveling in the first century, especially traveling preachers, avoided public inns with their pagan atmosphere and food that had already been offered to idols. Instead, they would seek out a Christian home in which to stop for the night. A valuable by-product of this practice was that believers from widely scattered areas would get to know one another, thus cementing lines of fellowship. Hospitality was a desperately needed virtue during that time.

We saw this method modeled by Jesus when He sent out the seventy.

> Carry no money belt, no bag, no shoes; and greet no
> one on the way. Whatever house you enter, first say,
> "Peace be to this house." If a man of peace is there, your

peace will rest on him; but if not, it will return to you. **Stay in that house**, eating and drinking what they give you; for the laborer is worthy of his wages. Do not keep moving from house to house. (Luke 10:4–7)

Later, traveling preachers and teachers who planted churches and ministered from city to city were often cared for by the local pastor of that village, town, or city. Hospitality in those times was a great and necessary virtue. Back then there were very few places of entertainment or public housing to host strangers.

In those days there wasn't a church building on every corner to choose from. The church was vulnerable in its early stage. Ancient churches had no church building in which to worship, and the normal practice was to meet in the home of a wealthy individual who had a home large enough to host a gathering. We see this in 1 Corinthians 16:19, "Aquila and Prisca greet you heartily in the Lord, with the church that is in their house" (see also Rom. 16:15; Col. 4:15).

The fledgling church of Christ relied heavily on hospitality to thrive. Her global expansion is due in part to men and women who showed hospitality to strangers.

The word used in 1 Timothy 3:2 is *philoxenia*, which is a compound word from two other Greek words: *philos*, which means "kind affection" or "love," and *xenos*, which means "stranger." *Philoxenia*—hospitality—means "to love strangers."[3]

Philoxenia, hospitality, then means being generous and caring for people we *do not* know. It is where we get the word *hospital*. Hospitals are where hurting people get help from strangers called doctors and nurses. The church is a hospital of sorts. It is a place where people find spiritual healing and meet one another's physical and emotional needs. Our homes, cars, and wallets should operate as mini hospitals too.

THE GIVING HOME

Several years ago, we invited a young man to live rent-free in our house for a season. We heard about his tragic story, and God moved us to action. Seven years after his adoption from Africa, his father raped him repeatedly. Finally, he mustered the courage to report his dad, who was sentenced to twenty years in prison. We met the young man shortly after the trial.

About a month after he moved in, he shared something we'd never thought twice about.

"This is a giving home," he observed.

"What are you talking about?" I asked.

"People are always doing stuff for you, and you are always doing things for other people. You are constantly giving stuff away to people, and they are often giving back to you. I've never seen anything like it before."

Several young men lived with us over the years. Giving was something we assumed Christians do habitually. At one point we remodeled our home to host more people. It was just something we've always done.

Theologian Henri Nouwen talked about hospitality from a unique perspective.

> Hospitality, therefore, means primarily the creation of a free space where a stranger can enter and become a friend instead of an enemy. Hospitality is not to change people, but to offer them space where change can take place.... The paradox of hospitality is that it wants to create emptiness ... where strangers can enter and

> discover themselves as created free; free to sing their
> own songs, speak their own languages, dance their own
> dances.... Hospitality is not a subtle invitation to adopt
> the life style of the host, but the gift of a chance for the
> guest to find his own.[4]

Hospitality invites people into its space, no strings attached, to be themselves, relaxed and free to enjoy the space they are in. Hospitality doesn't come with certain expectations or demands. Hospitality says, "Mi casa es su casa. Kick off your shoes and stay a while."

How many people feel this when they enter the antiseptic homes of believers who tell them to take off their shoes, keep their feet off the furniture, and put the toilet seat down after using it? Expectation and hospitality are enemies.

PHILOXENIA AND PHILEO

Hospitality is simple. Love people you do not know and welcome them into your space. If we've deconstructed what hospitality is not and determined what it is, then the pieces of the puzzle should fit immediately, right?

Wrong.

Phileo, sometimes translated as "highest form of love," is usually translated as "friendship" or "affection." Philadelphia has long been nicknamed the "City of Brotherly Love" because of the literal meaning of the city's name in Greek.

The foundation of hospitality is love.

That is what I love about the church. I once heard Mike Yaconelli joke that church is the place you go to hang out with people you don't like. I believe he meant that Christian love brings people together from all walks of life. It is the only place where I am close to men with whom I have little in common. Regarding hospitality, Gene Getz rightly observed, "True Christian love transcends economic status. And when it does not, it should."[5]

A HORRIFYING EPIPHANY

I want to close this chapter with a frightening warning from Jesus to those who, for whatever reason, reject the biblical mandate of hospitality in Matthew 25:41–45.

> Then he will say to those on his left, "Depart from me, you who are cursed, into the eternal fire prepared for the devil and his angels. For I was hungry and you gave me nothing to eat, I was thirsty and you gave me nothing to drink, I was a **stranger** and you did not invite me in, I needed clothes and you did not clothe me, I was sick and in prison and you did not look after me."

> They also will answer, "Lord, when did we see you hungry or thirsty or a stranger or needing clothes or sick or in prison, and did not help you?"

> He will reply, "Truly I tell you, whatever you did not do for one of the **least of these**, you did not do for me." (NIV)

Have you wondered why these church people were cursed to eternal separation from the God who "never knew" them (Matt. 7:23)? They failed to love people who were unknown to them—those who were hungry, thirsty, strangers, homeless, sick, and imprisoned—and loving people is the natural fruit of a regenerated life.

> Walk in Christ.
> Walk in love.
> Walk in hospitality.
> Walk close to strangers.
> And remember, "Mi casa es su casa."

DIAL IT IN
Small-Group Exercises

1. Read Titus 1:7–8 and 1 Timothy 3:2. How has your understanding of hospitality changed, and why is it so important for a man to be an example of it?

2. Which of the three misconceptions about hospitality ("Hospitality is not ...") was the most eye-opening to you, and why?

3. Why have some mistakenly thought hospitality is a spiritual gift? Why is this a cop-out? Read Romans 12:13, Hebrews 13:2, and 1 Peter 4:8–9.

4. What are some practical ways to show hospitality?

5. Look at Jesus' words about caring for the needy in Matthew 25:41–45 and the parable of the good Samaritan in Luke 10:25–37. What do they teach you about hospitality?

6. What new ways of expressing your faith will you put into practice because of this chapter?

ASSESSING YOUR CAPACITY

For each of the ten assessment statements, rank yourself accordingly:

(5) Strongly agree

(4) Agree

(3) Neither agree nor disagree

(2) Disagree

(1) Strongly disagree

Add up your total score at the bottom, then add the overall score in the appendix on page 281.

1. Blessing others in times of need makes me come alive. _____

I love to make people feel welcome. _____

I use my resources to bless others. _____

My neighbors stop by my house regularly. _____

I try to remember people's names. _____

People know they can borrow my stuff at any time. _____

I regularly introduce myself to strangers. _____

Mi casa es su casa ("My house is your house"). _____

People regularly come to my house to visit, hang out, or share a meal. _____

I look for opportunities to connect with people that I do not know well. _____

TOTAL SCORE _____

IO

THE GENEROUS MAN

You Can't Outgive God

Do all the good you can, by all the means you can, in all ways you can, in all the places you can, at all the times you can, to all the people you can, as long as you ever can.

—John Wesley

You have not lived today until you have done something for someone who can never repay you.

—John Bunyan

EYE OF THE NEEDLE

Matthew records a dialogue between Jesus and a man who is famously known as the rich young ruler. The young man had obvious good qualities, was wealthy, and was obedient to the Torah. But as Jesus dug deeper into his life, it became clear that God did not have all his life. God didn't have his wallet, and the man was unwilling to offer it up. The story ends with the rich young ruler walking away dejected and Jesus warning His listeners about wealth.

What did Jesus mean when He said, "It is easier for a camel to go through the eye of a needle, than for a rich man to enter the kingdom of God" (Matt. 19:24)?

Someone wise once said, "God doesn't have all your life until He has your wallet." Sadly, our resources are often the last items we offer up. If only we realized money's true value compared to eternity: "So we fix our eyes not on what is seen, but on what is unseen, since what is seen is temporary, but what is unseen is eternal" (2 Cor. 4:18 NIV).

Jesus' words, "eye of a needle," have great significance to a man I pray for regularly. He's a small-town farmer who is usually seen driving a muddy truck he never washes and wearing his customary Costco jeans and T-shirt. He would never stand out in the crowd as the full-throttle man that he is. And he prefers it that way. During a season when his fledgling business was starting to explode, he and his wife took a trip to the Holy Land. While touring, Jerusalem they stopped at the Sheep Gate at the Jerusalem wall. The Sheep Gate was the first gate to be restored by Nehemiah (Neh. 3:1), and it was the only gate that was set apart as holy since it was used for bringing in sacrifices for the temple. It was named the Sheep Gate because it was the entrance for sheep that were coming into the temple compound where lambs were sold for sacrifice and washed at the Pool of Bethesda (John 5:2).

Here's an interesting fact to ponder: except for the triumphal entry, Jesus always entered Jerusalem via the Sheep Gate.

"Behold the Lamb of God, which taketh away the sin of the world" (John 1:29 KJV).

For whatever reason, the day my friend visited it, the Sheep Gate was closed. Only the smaller gate for human passage was open. As my buddy stood there, a man walked up and tethered his donkey. The beast was fully loaded and unable to fit through the human door and had to be unloaded before moving through the small gap.

In that instant, my buddy heard the voice of God say, *If you unload your earthly wealth in this life, I will load you up in heaven.* It was a defining moment when my friend and his wife became two of the most systematically generous people I have ever met. He often quotes one of his favorite verses to me: "You do not have because you do not ask" (James 4:2). And it all started at the Sheep Gate in Jerusalem. He embodies the truth that you can't outgive God.

TWO NEGATIVES EQUAL ONE POSITIVE

People are strange when it comes to talking about money. Maybe it's because they're selfish and embarrassed by it. The most generous people I know are Jesus' followers. Conversely, the most selfish ones are not. Sadly, statistics show that most "Christians" give very little and are selfish and greedy, just like those outside the church.[1] I have no idea why. Those who are comfortable talking about money are often some of the most generous men I know. They don't share how much they give or to whom because they have a deep conviction of the treasure principle in Jesus' words.

> But when you give to the poor, do not let your left hand know what your right hand is doing, so that your giving will be in secret; and your Father who sees what is done in secret will reward you. (Matt. 6:3–4)

I wish more men would imitate the founder of the Methodist Church, John Wesley, who never lived on more than 30 British pounds a year. He consistently gave away the excess, even when his annual income reached as high as 1,400 pounds.[2] The message of his famous sermon entitled "The Use of Money" was basically make all you can, give all you can, save all you can.[3] The truth of generosity is also expressed in the Peace Prayer, commonly attributed to Francis of Assisi, which says, "For it is in giving that we receive."[4]

This chapter is unique because the Pastoral Epistles use two different negative words to make a point about generosity. In 1 Timothy 3:2–3, Paul used the Greek word *aphilarguron*, translated as "free from the love of money." The word is made up of *phileo*, "to be fond of," and *arguros*, "silver"—literally, "not a lover of silver."[5]

The only other time *aphilarguron* is mentioned in Scripture is Hebrews 13:5: "Make sure that your character is free from the love of money, being content with what you have."

John MacArthur described this kind of man as one who is "not ... greedy, stingy, or financially ambitious."[6] This dialed-in quality is an obvious reference to the commandment "You shall not covet your neighbor's house; you shall not covet your neighbor's wife or his male servant or his female servant or his ox or his donkey or anything that belongs to your neighbor" (Ex. 20:17).

Titus, however, uses the word *aischrokerdes*, translated as "not pursuing dishonest gain," which warns against being people who do not care how they make money as long as they make it (Titus 1:7 NIV).

About this quality Ray Pritchard wrote, "The godly leader must not make money the goal of his life. He must not be absorbed to increase his net worth."[7] Peter encouraged spiritual leaders, "Shepherd the flock of

God among you, exercising oversight not under compulsion, but voluntarily, according to the will of God; and not **for sordid gain**, but with eagerness" (1 Pet. 5:2).

Looking at the negative Greek words *aphilarguron* and *aischrokerdes,* we come up with one positive word: generous.

In other words, you can't outgive God.

THE RICH

I am rich. I have a house just for my tools—a shed. I have a fireproof room for my guns—a safe. My wife even has a room for her clothes—a walk-in closet. We have a separate room for food—a refrigerator. Even our car has a home of its own—a garage. Millions of our Christian brothers and sisters worldwide don't have any of these things but still live joyful, content, and generous lives.

We grow plants we don't eat. We have water that runs, sewage that is flushed, lights that come on with the click of a switch, food we throw away, air temperatures we control. Even our pets eat better than many humans. We are so rich that when my wife says, "I have nothing to wear," she means, "I have nothing *new* to wear!"

We are the people Paul warned in 1 Timothy 6:6–10:

> But godliness with contentment is great gain. For we brought nothing into the world, and we can take nothing out of it. But if we have food and clothing, we will be content with that. Those who want to get rich fall into temptation and a trap and into many foolish and harmful desires that plunge people into ruin and destruction. For the **love of money** is a root of all kinds

of evil. Some people, eager for money, have wandered
from the faith and pierced themselves with many griefs.
(NIV)

The problem is twofold. First, we compare our wealth to that of those
around us instead of those around the world. Second, we do not obey the
Bible's teaching about wealth. If your toilet flushes, your lights magically
click on, and you have special rooms for possessions, you are living in
the world of the wealthy. Ecclesiastes 5:10 offers another warning to the
greedy, "He who loves money will not be satisfied with money, nor he who
loves abundance with its income."

It is not the rich who are the problem. It is not money that is the
problem either. It is the "love of money"—when money comes before
trusting Jesus. If you follow Jesus yet refuse to tithe, it is either because
you are ignorant (no one told you) or idolatrous (you love money more
than Jesus). The former is no longer an excuse. Remember Paul's words in
1 Timothy 6:17–19 about whom to put our hope in and how that hope
manifests to the world.

Command those who are rich in this present world
not to be arrogant nor to put their hope in wealth,
which is so uncertain, but to put their hope in God,
who richly provides us with everything for our enjoy-
ment. Command them to do good, to be rich in good
deeds, and to be generous and willing to share. In this
way they will lay up treasure for themselves as a firm
foundation for the coming age, so that they may take
hold of the life that is truly life. (NIV)

My organization, Men in the Arena, strives to be generous, offering the electronic version of our resources for free to missionaries, active military, men in underdeveloped nations, first responders, and men who are incarcerated. If you own a hard copy of this book, congratulations. You are rich! Now that we've determined that most of us are indeed wealthy, let's dive into some tips for being generous with our wealth.

One of the many stories that stand out in Ramos family lore happened in Sunriver, Oregon, on Thanksgiving weekend when we decided to give our busy single-mom waitress a 100 percent tip for working so hard away from her children on a holiday. We had a blast leaving all that money. It was the perfect way to teach my sons that you can't outgive God. Here are some tips you can implement to test whether you can outgive God. (You can't.)

Give expecting a greater reward. I've tithed out of obedience since early on in my Christian journey, but I want to return to what my buddy learned that day in Jerusalem. You can't outgive God. Paul shared a powerful message to the church at Philippi, "You yourselves also know, Philippians, that at the first preaching of the gospel, after I left Macedonia, no church shared with me in the matter of giving and receiving but you alone; for even in Thessalonica you sent a gift more than once for my needs. Not that I seek the gift itself, but I seek for the profit which **increases** to your account" (Phil. 4:15–17).

I can't outgive God because every time I give, I not only bless the ministries I support but increase my eternal wealth as well! It is a win-win for God's kingdom.

Give as budgeted, no questions asked. Our giving is budgeted after prayer and careful consideration. Our giving checks are the first checks that we send.

Give the first 10 percent (at least), no questions asked. In other words, budget off the top. Contrary to Scripture, some financial "experts" tell their followers to pay yourself first. I disagree. Instead, you should pay God first. We've done this our entire marriage, even when we were so broke that we struggled to pay bills. We tithed as an offering of trust and obedience. God never failed to meet our needs.

Give the 10 percent to kingdom-minded ministries. In Romans 1:16, Paul said, "I am not ashamed of the gospel of Christ" (KJV). I personally do not give my firstfruits to any organization that's not overtly Christian, even if it's run by believers. This is God's money we are dealing with, not mine. I will not give, no matter how honorable the cause, my top 10 percent unless it is an unashamedly kingdom-minded organization, such as a church, faith-based ministry, or missionary.

Give cheerfully. In the two local churches I worked in, I was required to give a storehouse tithe to the church before giving above and beyond to other ministries or missionaries, which we did faithfully for two decades. But storehouse tithing is never commanded in the New Testament. Instead, 2 Corinthians 9:7 gives a different pattern, telling us that "God loves a cheerful giver," who gives "just as he has purposed in his heart, not grudgingly or under compulsion." We give our first 10 percent to the kingdom-focused ministries we care about and those that give us great joy.

Let your children give. I cannot stress this enough if your children are in your home. Do not give online. You are leading a family. You are training your children to live, like you, at full capacity. Let your children see, touch, and physically give the checks, whether they put the money into an offering basket or a stamped envelope.

Give above 10 percent as God prompts, no questions asked. Two months ago, our son Colton moved back into our home for a couple of months after graduating with his bachelor's degree. He was so thankful for living rent-free under our roof that last week he surprised us by replacing our decade-old forty-seven-inch television with a sixty-five-inch monster! We were so blessed, not by the sweet new big screen, but by the fact that our amazing son is learning this sacred truth: you can't outgive God.

Give to the God who can't be outgiven. Throw out the Greek words you learned in this chapter. Throw out your opinion about what groups should be given to and how much they should get. Generosity comes down to one thing. Do you trust God before all things? Does He have all of you—including your wallet?

And remember, you can't outgive God.

DIAL IT IN
Small-Group Exercises

1. If you were preaching a three-point sermon on giving based on the story of the rich young ruler in Matthew 19:16–30, what would be your main teaching points?

2. Read 1 Timothy 3:3, 1 Timothy 6:10, and Hebrews 13:5. How do you know when money becomes idolatrous?

3. Discuss this statement: "Do all the good you can, by all the means you can, in all ways you can, in all the places you can, at all the times you can, to all the people you can, as long as you ever can."

4. What is a correct eternal perspective of wealth according to Deuteronomy 8:17–18, Psalm 50:9–10, and 2 Corinthians 4:18?

5. What do Luke 16:9 and 2 Corinthians 9:7 teach us about generosity?

6. Which of the eight tips for giving is the most difficult for you to believe? Why?

7. Which is the most difficult to practice? Why?

ASSESSING YOUR CAPACITY

For each of the ten assessment statements, rank yourself accordingly:

> (5) Strongly agree
>
> (4) Agree
>
> (3) Neither agree nor disagree
>
> (2) Disagree
>
> (1) Strongly disagree

Add up your total score at the bottom, then add the overall score in the appendix on page 283.

1. I give at least 10 percent of my income to the causes I care about. _____

I am known as a generous man. _____

Carrying consumer debt is not a wise principle to live by. _____

I give without expecting anything in return. _____

I am not motivated by the love of money. _____

I never cheat or lie just to accumulate wealth. _____

I am not thought of as a hoarder. _____

I regularly give more than expected. _____

I live by the truth that "God loves a cheerful giver" (2 Cor. 9:7). _____

I firmly believe that it is better to give than to receive. _____

TOTAL SCORE _____

THE GOOD MAN

No More Mr. Nice Guy

Associate yourself with people of good quality,
for it is better to be alone than in bad company.

Nice people cannot and do not contend with injustice and its
corresponding evil. Good people do.

—Paul Coughlin, *No More Christian Nice Guy*

THE QUESTION MEN ASK

Saving Private Ryan is one of my all-time favorite movies. The movie was
based off Max Allan Collins's book of the same title. Set in France days
after the June 6, 1944, invasion of German-occupied France during World
War II, it tracks a group of soldiers on their mission to locate Private
James Francis Ryan and bring him home safely after his three brothers are
killed in action.

The movie is loosely based on the story of the four Niland brothers who served in the military during World War II. Ultimately, two brothers survived the war, but for a while, only Fritz Niland was believed to have survived and was sent back to the United States to complete his service. Later it was discovered that his brother Edward, who was missing and presumed dead, was alive and held captive by the Japanese.

The movie ends with a ferocious combat sequence and a mortally wounded Captain Miller, who, moments before his death, utters to Private Ryan, "James, earn this. Earn it."[1] His final words were a grim reminder that many had lost their lives to save him, so he should live in a way that showed his life was worth saving. He must never take his life for granted.

The next scene shows a much older James Ryan, accompanied by his loving family, standing next to the gravesite of Captain Miller and speaking with emotion about the life Captain Miller and others had saved—and Private Ryan had lived. His profound words hit hard and resonate with the souls of men:

> My family is with me today. They wanted to come with me. To be honest with you, I wasn't sure how I'd feel coming back here. Every day I think about what you said to me that day on the bridge. I tried to live my life the best that I could. I hope that was enough. I hope that, at least in your eyes, I've earned what all of you have done for me.[2]

His wife then approaches to comfort him, and Ryan asks her to tell him what all men want to hear:

"Tell me I've led a good life."

"What?"

"Tell me I'm a good man."

Then Ryan's wife gives him the answer every man wants to hear from those he loves:

"You are."[3]

You are. You are a good man. This video clip was shown at a men's getaway weekend for the church I attend, and—unbeknownst to others—it wrecked my friend Kirt, who is an exemplary servant at our church. Weeping at church the next day, he could barely communicate what God had done to affirm that he was indeed a good man.

I now call him "Kirt the Good" as a constant reminder of how his friends and family see him. I'm convinced that men are striving to be good. Our souls long to be recognized for some good we have done in life. Many find their identity in work because it's the one thing they are good at. We long to be called good. I've never met a man who wanted to be known as worthless, bad, or anonymous.

As Henry David Thoreau reflected, "Goodness is the only investment that never fails."[4] My goals for this chapter are for us to understand what it means to be a lover of good, to repent of niceness when it contradicts goodness, and to hate the evils of this world.

But what is so bad about being nice? Isn't niceness a Christian virtue?

NO MORE MR. NICE GUY

No.

Niceness is most definitely not a Christian virtue.

The word *nice* is nowhere to be found in the Bible. The ancient Jews as a people, and Israel as a nation, were considered insolent, violent, and aggressive by their enemies (Ezra 4:19). They were constantly at war. They were never known as "nice."

There is a prevailing belief among the misinformed that Jesus didn't drink, get angry, use sarcasm, confront people, ask awkward questions, grow impatient, or complain. The Bible proves that He did all the above without apology, confession, or repentance (Heb. 4:15).

The word *nice* began as a negative term derived from the Latin *nescius*, meaning "unaware or ignorant." This sense of "ignorant" was carried over into English when the word was first borrowed from Latin in the early 1300s. For almost a century after that, *nice* was used to characterize a stupid, ignorant, or foolish person.[5] It finds its roots in the word *ignore*.

The nice guy chooses to ignore or be uninformed about battling the evils of this world even though Jesus said, "From the days of John the Baptist until now the kingdom of heaven suffers violence, and violent men take it by force" (Matt. 11:12). I wonder where Mr. Nice Guy fits in the narrative of disrupting the kingdom of darkness with light.

Brennan Manning made this observation: "Preoccupation with projecting the 'nice guy' image ... leads to self-consciousness, sticky pedestal behavior, and unfreedom in the iron grip of human respect."[6]

Paul Coughlin offers this insight about when evil threatens good: "Nice people actually oppose good people who rock the boat, even when headed toward God's will.... Nice people cannot and do not contend with injustice and its corresponding evil. Good people do."[7]

He accurately describes nice guys as "low wattage, tepid, timid, fearful, anxious. But they're really nice," and he goes on to say, "Jesus' behavior was so different from how the average guy in a church is expected to behave that if you look at the record honestly, we wouldn't pray **to** such a person. We would pray **for** such a person!"[8]

Mr. Nice Guy lives small and anonymously and believes that if he keeps his mouth shut, everything will work out just fine. Mr. Nice Guy is a peacefaker (see chapter 7). Martin Luther King Jr. said about people who failed to act, "History will have to record that the greatest tragedy of this period of social transition was not the strident clamor of the bad people, but the appalling silence of the good people."[9]

No more Mr. Nice Guy.

GOOD COMPARISONS

Speaking of Jesus, I'm reminded of a conversation Jesus had with someone who thought he was pretty good.

> As He was setting out on a journey, a man ran up to Him and knelt before Him, and asked Him, "Good Teacher, what shall I do to inherit eternal life?" And Jesus said to him, "Why do you call Me good? No one is good except God alone." (Mark 10:17–18)

In a recent premarital counseling session with a nonchurch couple, the topic of God came up, and the intelligent bride-to-be described her spirituality as "I am a good person who tries to do what is right."

Her statement of faith compelled me to show her the misdirection of her moral compass: "What do you base your definition of good on? If you compare yourself to most of humanity, you may be right. You are a good person. But if your moral absolute of good is based on a perfect and holy

God, then you are a wretched, vile creature who does not measure up to any standard of good."

"I never thought of it that way," she confessed. "I need to think through what you said."

The Bible rightfully declares, "All have turned away, they have together become worthless; there is **no one** who does good, **not even one**. 'Their throats are open graves; their tongues practice deceit'" (Rom. 3:12–13 NIV).

More information is at our fingertips than ever before, yet truth eludes us. We've become ethically apathetic, morally confused, and biblically ignorant. We describe absolutes as "my truth" instead of *the* truth. To obtain an accurate bearing, we must compare our moral standards with the character and nature of God and the Bible's teachings.

For example, abortion is one of the greatest evils of our day, where millions of innocents have been murdered in the name of convenience. But many would disagree, calling it a good choice. A prevailing thought in colonial America was that slavery was good and beneficial, but most would agree today that slavery is the horrible objectification of people made in God's image. We can go on and on.

I live by the motto that the majority is usually wrong and that we will always be surrounded by godless people who believe popular culture is moral truth.

HATE IS A STRONG WORD—HATE ANYWAY

There is a prevailing lie in the church today that warns against getting angry, losing our cool, and—God help us—hating. Because love is the greatest Christian virtue and included in both the Great Commandments in Matthew 22:37–40 (see also 1 Cor. 13:13), we wrongly deduce that hate should be eradicated. But in Malachi 2:16, God says, "I hate divorce," because He sees the destruction caused by the death of a marriage through divorce.

There are many favorable mentions of hatred in the Bible, usually a hatred of evil, but even hatred of evildoers. For example, speaking of evil, the psalmist said of God, "You hate all who do iniquity" (Ps. 5:5).

In Titus 1:7–8, we read, "For the overseer must be above reproach ... loving what is good." The Greek word used is *philagathos*, "which means either someone who loves **good things** or who loves **good people** ... that is, someone who loves **good actions**."[10] We cannot love something without loathing—hating—anything that opposes it. To love marriage is to hate divorce. To love good is to hate evil. To love God is to hate Satan.

Philagathos is a compound word from the Greek *phileo* ("to love") and *agathos* ("good"); combined, these words describe a lover of good. But what exactly does good (*agathos*) mean? How do we define *good* biblically? According to W. E. Vine, *agathos* "describes that which, being good in its character or constitution, is beneficial in its effect."[11] In other words, true goodness comes from a heart like God's, and it works for the true benefit of others. Note well that when you do something good for the benefit of others, it won't necessarily be nice, and other people may not appreciate the good you have done!

In 2 Timothy 3:1–5, Paul used the antithesis of *philagathos* to describe those who oppose the gospel:

> But realize this, that in the last days difficult times will come. For men will be **lovers** of self, **lovers** of money, boastful, arrogant, revilers, disobedient to parents, ungrateful, unholy, unloving, irreconcilable, malicious

gossips, without self-control, brutal, haters of good
[*aphilagathos*], treacherous, reckless, conceited, **lovers** of pleasure rather than lovers of God, holding to a
form of godliness, although they have denied its power;
Avoid such men as these.

Paul warned that we should avoid any person who hates good (*aphilagathos*). He would agree that we should also confront those who oppose
good when God provides opportunities to do so. To avoid such an opportunity is cowardice disguised as godliness. Paul was compelled to do this
when Peter threatened the good expansion of the gospel to Gentiles by
trying to implement Jewish law as a requisite of faith: "But when Cephas
[Peter] came to Antioch, I opposed him to his face, because he stood
condemned. For prior to the coming of certain men from James, he used
to eat with the Gentiles; but when they came, he began to withdraw and
hold himself aloof, fearing the party of the circumcision" (Gal. 2:11–12).

No more Mr. Nice Guy when it comes to the evils of this world. Evil
reigns when good men go soft in the face of anything that opposes good.

My mother contracted German measles while pregnant with my
brother and was told to abort him because he had a high probability of
being born with severe disabilities. My Grandpa Ramos, a chain-smoker,
made a deal with God that, if my brother was born healthy, he would quit
smoking. On September 26, 1967, my mother gave birth to a healthy baby
boy. It was the last time my grandpa smoked a cigarette. Not only did he
quit, but he developed a deep loathing for cigarettes, tobacco smoke, and
anything related. His hatred fueled his oath to the Lord.

The prophet Amos reminds us to "hate evil, love good" (Amos 5:15).

Hate is a powerful tool for the man committed to loving good. In his book *Dangerous Good*, Kenny Luck wrote, "The man of God is not a spectator to God's Kingdom purposes being advanced on earth. God never intended His sons to watch the battle between evil and good; He expects us to fight for the good of our faith—in the open."[12]

Good men fight against evil because they stand diametrically opposed to anything that blocks the path of doing good. Believers are told, "Do not be overcome by evil, but overcome evil with good" (Rom. 12:21). And again to "hate what is evil; cling to what is good" (Rom. 12:9 NIV). Some credit German philosopher Friedrich Wilhelm Nietzsche with saying this about the tension between nice and good: "Niceness is what is left of goodness when it is drained of greatness."

Even Voltaire, a staunch antagonist of Christianity, is thought to have argued "every man is guilty of all the good he **did not** do." William Barclay defined *philagathos* as "a word which means either someone who loves good things or who loves good people and good actions."[13]

Let's explore what these three—good things, good people, and good actions—represent in the context of loving what is good.

GOOD THINGS

In C. S. Lewis's *The Lion, the Witch and the Wardrobe*, Susan learns about Christ's representation, Aslan, from Mr. Beaver, who says, "Aslan is a lion—the Lion, the great Lion."

"Ooh," said Susan. "I'd thought he was a man. Is he—quite safe? I shall feel rather nervous about meeting a lion."

"Safe?" asked Mr. Beaver. "Who said anything about safe? 'Course he isn't safe. But he's good."[14]

In Mark 10:17–18 we see something similar, "As He [Jesus] was setting out on a journey, a man ran up to Him and knelt before Him, and asked Him, 'Good Teacher, what shall I do to inherit eternal life?' And Jesus said to him, 'Why do you call Me good? No one is good except God alone.'"

Aslan and Jesus are good because their nature demands loving everything good. Chapter 5 challenged you to take everything in moderation, imitating the apostle Paul, who said, "All things are lawful for me, but not all things are profitable. All things are lawful for me, but I will not be mastered by anything" (1 Cor. 6:12).

Even good things become bad when they have mastery over our lives. It is simple to hate the evils of our world like abortion, genocide, and racial favoritism, but it is more difficult to navigate the gray waters of moderation.

I'm regularly challenged to regulate what nutrients I ingest, how I pursue my calling, and what hobbies and pleasures I enjoy so that a good thing doesn't turn into a bad thing.

Everything has the potential to damage and must be monitored ruthlessly.

GOOD PEOPLE

I've been in vocational ministry since 1990, so hear me when I say that the people you choose as your inner circle will either make or break your life. The saying is true. You are nothing more than the average of the five people you spend the most time with. I have seen teens from godly families who sheltered their children in a homeschool environment fall away from the things of God because of one bad relationship. Paul was right when he warned, "Do not be deceived: 'Bad company corrupts good morals'" (1 Cor. 15:33).

Conversely, I have seen students from broken dysfunctional backgrounds live in victory because they found salvation in Jesus and fell in love with the local church. The most vibrant, dynamic Christian men I know are fully engaged in a local community of believers. Why am I plugged into a local church? I love good. And the body of Christ is good.

Hebrews 10:23–25 admonishes those who have strayed:

> Let us hold fast the confession of our hope without wavering, for He who promised is faithful; and let us consider how to stimulate one another to love and good deeds, not forsaking our own assembling together, as is the habit of some, but encouraging one another; and all the more as you see the day drawing near.

Experience has taught that Christian fellowship is the first thing to go when a man backslides. It is also the first thing to implement when a man moves to full capacity.

Booker T. Washington is one of my heroes. His autobiography is inspiring. Washington was an American educator and adviser to several US presidents between 1890 and 1915 and a leader in the African American community. He accomplished what many would have deemed impossible for that day and age. He is widely credited with echoing the commonly held wisdom of his time: "Associate yourself with people of good quality, for it is better to be alone than in bad company."

The Association Principle is simple yet profound: you will become like those you hang out with. Someone who was addicted to methamphetamine once told me, "Everyone I know does meth."

I responded, "That is weird, because you are the only person I know who does it."

Today she is free, and nobody she knows does meth. Interesting.

John F. Kennedy is often quoted as saying, "A rising tide lifts all ships." Conversely, a receding tide lowers all ships. My friendships are strictly utilitarian. I live a full life. Every moment is precious and cannot be redeemed. If a friend does not lift me in some way, I stop spending time with them. They move into the acquaintance category. I am cordial but not invested. This may sound harsh, but unless people are immediate family members, I am not accountable for their lives, just mine. If you want to run with horses (Jer. 12:5), you need to stop running with asses. If you want to soar with eagles, you need to get out of the chicken coop.

Do you think it was a coincidence that Jesus waited until Judas left the upper room before instructing the remaining disciples on the importance of love? He said, "A new commandment I give to you, that you love one another, even as I have loved you, that you also love one another. By this all men will know that you are My disciples, if you have love for one another" (John 13:31, 34–35).

Do the right thing. Get the right men in your life. Get rid of the bad. No more Mr. Nice Guy.

GOOD ACTIONS

Earlier you learned that Theodore Roosevelt, while enrolled at Harvard, was removed as a Sunday school teacher for rewarding a student who stood up to a bully. Roosevelt, who read his Bible daily and attended church weekly, observed that there were men who "were very nice, very refined, who shook their heads over political corruption and discussed it in drawing-rooms and parlors, but who were wholly unable to grapple with real men in real life."[15]

In other words, they were intellectually sharp but weak and soft and could not keep pace with what Roosevelt called "real men." The church rewards nice, refined, intellectual men and is intimidated by men who are hands-on, blue-collar, and rougher around the edges. We've bought the lie that goodness and niceness are synonymous.

This couldn't be further from the truth. Some of the nicest guys I know are like those Roosevelt observed over a century ago—worthless, gutless, and anonymous. I've seen churches destroyed at the hands of gutless cowards who blamed God for their silence.

How do I know? It takes one to know one.

Addressing church artwork, John Eldredge observed, "Yes, those are the pictures I've seen myself in many churches. In fact, those are the only pictures I've seen of Jesus. They leave me with the impression that he was the world's nicest guy. Mister Rogers with a beard. Telling me to be like him feels like telling me to go limp and passive. Be nice. Be swell.... I'd much rather be told to be like William Wallace."[16]

Last week, after church, I thought about a metal chair with green cushions that is at my house. It was the chair my buddy Glenn hauled in the back of his truck everywhere he went. Three months ago, he died of a massive heart attack. We recently installed a park bench with his name on it. His chair stays at my house, a reminder of what it means to be a good man.

I'm not sure if I ever saw Glenn without his denim bib overalls, even on our whitewater rafting trips. He smoked too much. He ate too much bacon. He was loud, obnoxious, and intimidating at times. No one would describe him as nice. And yet people flooded into his memorial service at the height of the pandemic. Hundreds. Why all the commotion over such an unrefined redneck?

Glenn was good.

Churches are filled today with nameless, faceless, anonymous men who show up week after week and never do anything but smile nicely and waste space. When they leave, no one cares or notices. Act where others watch passively. Get out of the anonymous bleachers and into the arena.

No more Mr. Nice Guy.

DIAL IT IN
Small-Group Exercises

1. Where has being nice become your Achilles' heel? What will you do about it?

2. Compare good and evil in 2 Timothy 3:1–5 and Titus 1:7–8. What insights do you find there?

3. How do the lives of those who hate good differ from those who love it?

4. Compare Amos 5:15, Romans 12:9, and Romans 12:2. What role does hate play in loving good?

5. Why are John 13:31–35 and Hebrews 10:23–25 so important for the dialed in man? How can you build a healthier relationship with a community of believers?

6. What other insights about good versus evil can you find in Psalm 97:10 and Proverbs 8:13?

7. What bad relationships do you need to replace?

ASSESSING YOUR CAPACITY

For each of the ten assessment statements, rank yourself accordingly:

> (5) Strongly agree
>
> (4) Agree
>
> (3) Neither agree nor disagree
>
> (2) Disagree
>
> (1) Strongly disagree

Add up your total score at the bottom, then add the overall score in the appendix on page 284.

1. I long for the things that please God. _____

I always do what is morally right. _____

I refuse to watch or listen to any content that will not make me better. _____

I strictly monitor what I watch and listen to. _____

I would rather be known as a good man than a nice man. _____

I would rather be good than look good. _____

I look for the best in every situation. _____

I always see the goodness in other people. _____

I refuse to engage in any behavior that might tempt my heart away from Jesus. _____

I believe that our worst messes can become our greatest message. _____

TOTAL SCORE _____

THE DEVOUT MAN

Religiously Practicing Your Faith

On the day of judgment, surely, we shall not be asked what we have read, but what we have done; not how well we have spoken, but how well we have lived.

—Thomas à Kempis, *The Imitation of Christ*

God works most effectively through holy men.

—E. M. Bounds, *The Essentials of Prayer*

RELIGIOUS ABOUT YOUR RELATIONSHIP

In college, I suffered a life-changing knee injury. Minutes into anterior cruciate ligament reconstructive surgery, during which I was accidentally overdosed by my anesthesiologist, I went into anaphylactic shock. When I came back to consciousness, I couldn't breathe or see, but I could hear the frantic orders from my surgeon and the rapidly increasing beeping of the heart rate monitor to my left.

"He's going Code Blue!"—cardiac arrest—someone shouted.

I thought, *Someone in this room is really in trouble*, only to realize that someone was me!

My throat was swollen shut, so I couldn't talk. My eyes were also swollen shut, so I couldn't see. When I began losing the ability to breathe, I started to panic. In a moment of clarity, however, I decided to communicate the letters H-E-L-P with my arms. But everyone in the room thought I was having a seizure. As I flailed, tiny nurses tried to restrain me. It must have been quite a scene!

An injection of adrenaline calmed the anaphylactic reaction and brought my heart rate down.

"He's going to be okay," the doctor tried to reassure my parents. "I think."

That didn't help. I slowly recovered in the intensive care unit (ICU), but my eyes remained swollen shut until the third day.

That's when it happened. I heard the definitive voice of God for the first time. My mom must have walked into the ICU at the same moment because she noticed an invisible Presence in the room as God whispered to her, "He's mine now." She left the room in tears, thinking I was about to die.

What happened next changed my life. Ruined it. Wrecked it. And in the process made it beautiful, unique, and worth living.

"I want you to make a difference in the lives of teens." I was nineteen.

It was a call to ministry, but I wouldn't realize it until years later. Next quarter, I changed my major from business to psychology and began volunteering with teens on the autism spectrum. A few years later, I entered vocational ministry where I have been ever since.

Blinded in the ICU, I was called by God for His purposes, but He called me to more than ministry. He called me to Him, to be set apart for Him. His immediate purposes are secondary to being set apart for Him. Living a devout and holy life starts with consecration, which E. M. Bounds called "the human side of holiness."[1]

What do you think of when you hear the words *devout* and *holy*? Gary Thomas put it this way: "Many of us think of holiness in terms of what we don't do.... Jesus taught a positive ethic—what matters most, he said, is what we do do."[2]

The truth is that a devout man does and does not do certain things. He is a beautiful blend of discipline and freedom. Being holy means making choices against anything hindering God's work in you so that you can live fully devoted to Him. The devout life is one of balance between doing what is good and pleasing to God and shunning those things that are not.

I love the bluntness of E. M. Bounds. He wrote, "God must have men in their entirety. No double-minded man need apply. No vacillating man can be used.... Holiness is wholeness, and so God wants holy men, men whole-hearted and true."[3]

John Wesley knew the value of men with such a deep conviction. He said, "Give me one hundred preachers who fear nothing but sin, and desire nothing but God, and I care not a straw whether they be clergymen or laymen; such alone will shake the gates of hell and set up the kingdom of heaven on Earth."[4]

God wants to put men on display, but it is the devout who will shine the brightest for God and give Him the glory for it. They are the ones who are walking with God in all areas of devotion.

Get religious (about your relationship) with God.

LIVING RELIGIOUSLY

A gray bow case sits on the top shelf in my garage from the end of archery season in late September until sometime in the late spring. I love to hunt but am what some would call an archery opportunist—not a purist by any means. Mind and muscle memory are vital for successful archers; many will practice every day of the week, all year long. They do it religiously.

Sometime in late spring, I will begin shooting my bow with the goal of shooting fifteen arrows a day, every day of the week, leading up to the opening day of archery season in late August. Think about this commitment—shooting nearly two thousand practice arrows in the four months leading up to that one opportunity. Archers practice because they love their sport. They do it to make every opportunity count. They do it because they know success means practicing their craft religiously.

The same holds true for anything or anyone you love. They do it religiously.

The Greek word Paul uses in Titus 1:8 is *hosios*, meaning "pious" or "devout"; it suggests being faithful in all one's duties to God.[5] But it is much more than that. It is having or showing deep religious feelings or commitment.[6] The devout man embodies three things in line with *hosios*. First, his life is associated with righteousness. Second, his life is set apart for God as opposed to what is unrighteous or polluted. Third, *hosios* describes his distinct Christian character.[7] The threefold purpose of *hosios*, then, is doing certain things in line with personal piety, being obedient to what is pleasing to God, and being consistent with religious practices.[8]

According to these explanations, the devout man who is living religiously practices three things.

BIBLICAL OBEDIENCE

For centuries European royalty displayed their regalia with beautiful white fur with striking black tail tips, fur from the short-tailed weasel, or ermine, found in the northernmost parts of North America.

The ermine's fur turns from a milk-chocolate color in the summer to the whitest of whites in the winter. Its extreme aversion to dirt is its downfall. Hunters know this. Whenever an ermine burrow is discovered, hunters line it with feces, then send the hounds to pick up the ermine's scent. Once spotted, the ermine escapes to its honey hole, only to realize it has been contaminated with excrement. Being obsessed with a clean coat, the ermine will fight to the death instead of staining its precious coat.

Its instinct for purity outweighs its survival instinct.

As we look at the word *devout*, also translated as *holy*, consider the ermine and its obsession with purity. God wants strong men who hate sin and long to set themselves apart for His purposes, not soft men who fall prey to every whim or urge. Jerry Bridges wrote, "Holiness is not an option but a must for every Christian."[9] J. Oswald Sanders would have concurred; he believed that "happiness is a by-product of holiness."[10]

The devout man understands that grace is free. But it isn't cheap. It's disturbing to see how morally similar "Christian" men are to those outside the church. I am appalled at how an engaged "Christian" man can show no regard for biblical purity before marriage. He can cohabitate, have premarital sex, and parade his fiancée at church on Sunday as if nothing is wrong. Instead of protecting her like the priceless queen she is, he parades her like a cheap harlot. I'm shocked at the alcohol abuse, gluttony, and laziness of these same men.

What's happened to the devout men of the church? Where have they gone? Have they taken grace for granted, or has the church just gotten so soft and weak that men are unwilling to fight to live a devout and holy life? The church has made it too easy to be spiritually soft, weak, and non-compliant with Scripture.

"What shall we say then? Are we to continue in sin so that grace may increase? May it never be! How shall we who died to sin still live in it?" (Rom. 6:1–2). Living in unrepentant sin is choosing to walk away from God, not with God, but the devout man is committed to personal holiness through biblical obedience. I love how Peter said it: "Like the Holy One who called you, be holy yourselves also in all your behavior; because it is written, 'You shall be holy, for I am holy'" (1 Pet. 1:15–16).

SERVING OTHERS IN JESUS' NAME

We moved to Oregon towing a spray-painted green 1983 Ford Bronco. A few of the men at church lamented that it was not suitable for a guy of my status. One day they surprised me with a beautiful truck that came with a card that quoted Philippians 2:3–4: "Do nothing from selfishness or empty conceit, but with humility of mind regard one another as more important than yourselves; do not merely look out for your own personal interests, but also for the interests of others."

In other words, the Christian man must serve others with his gifts, talents, and resources. Galatians 5:13 teaches, "Through love serve one another." Peter said something similar, "As each one has received a special gift, employ it in serving one another as good stewards of the manifold grace of God" (1 Pet. 4:10).

Christian service is the fruit of a devout and holy life. The very definition of holiness is "set apart for God's purposes." How can a man claim to follow Jesus yet refuse to set himself apart for God to serve others? Mother Teresa, the fierce servant of India's downtrodden, is believed to have said, "Not all of us can do great things, but we can do small things with great love." Love and service are two sides of the same coin.

Both churches I worked in throughout my two decades of local church ministry had similar slogans about Christian service. The first was "Every Christian is a minister, and every minister has a ministry." The other is like it: "Every minister—a ministry."

One can't be devoted to Jesus without being devoted to others. Love God. Love people. It is that simple. How do you measure your devotion to the things of God? Years ago, an experience with the pastor who married Shanna and me inspired me to ask, "What does it mean to be a devout follower of Jesus? What does it mean to walk with God?"

WALKING WITH GOD

I was driving home from freshman basketball practice with my coach, Gary McCusker, when I first heard it. Four years later, he would lead me to Jesus, partly because of what he shared that day.

In his usual invasive way, he launched into a forced presentation of the gospel, and I stopped him midsentence. "Gary, I agree with all that you are telling me, but I will never go to church again."

I had attended regularly as a child but was bored out of my young mind.

He calmly responded, "Jim, Christianity is not about church or religion but having a relationship with God through Jesus Christ."

It was a mic-drop moment.

Are you telling me that I can have a relationship with God and never have to go to church? Ever?

It wasn't soon after giving my life to Jesus that I found my way into a local church, and I've worked in churches for two decades and lived at a church parsonage nearly half that time! God certainly has a sense of humor.

I have been attending church religiously my entire adult life. Why? Because it is one of several things I do to grow in my relationship with my Creator. Let me explain.

In Genesis, we read about an obscure man named Enoch. As quickly as he appears in Scripture, he vanishes—literally! Genesis records his unique relationship with God, "Then Enoch **walked with God** three hundred years after he became the father of Methuselah, and he had other sons and daughters.... Enoch walked with God; and he was not, for God took him" (5:22–24).

In my journey with Jesus, since the late 1980s, I have religiously practiced seven disciplines, using *walking* as a mnemonic device. Measure your spiritual devotion against them.

Worship God consistently. There are eleven words for worship in the New Testament, but the Greek word *proskuneo* is mentioned more times than all the other ten words combined! *Proskuneo* means, "To kiss, like a dog licking his master's hand; to fawn or crouch to, prostrate oneself in homage (do reverence to—adore)- worship.[11]

Where do you go to kiss the nail-scarred hands of Jesus? Where do you go to sit at His feet (no licking in church, please)? Worship is how we express our deep devotion to the Savior. I find my local church is the best place to worship God. Corporate worship is an invaluable conduit for these expressions of devotion.

Approach God through a blocked time of prayer. Jesus set the example for prayer, sneaking away from the crowds regularly to pray. He had specific times He'd pray (Mark 1:35; 14:32; Luke 5:16; 11:1). Before teaching His disciples how to pray (Matt. 6:9–13), He encouraged them to set a time and place: "But you, when you pray, go into your inner room, close your door and pray to your Father who is in secret, and your Father who sees what is done in secret will reward you" (Matt. 6:6).

Love other believers through consistent fellowship. Journey with me to the dusty corner of the upper room the night before the crucifixion. Noticed the strategically placed candles. See the thirteen pairs of sandals airing out on the floor. Smell the musk of a dozen men after the heat of the day. Step over the basin filled with dirty water. In the corner is the dirty towel Jesus used on the disciples' feet.

Can you imagine the tension in the room that night? Jesus was fighting back His fears of impending doom and His tears because of His friend's imminent betrayal. Judas was looking for the perfect moment to betray Jesus. Undiscussed anxiety filled the upper room.

Judas left on his mission of betrayal, and Jesus spoke, "A new commandment I give to you, that you love one another, even as I have loved you, that you also love one another. **By this** all men will know that you are My disciples, if you have love for one another" (John 13:34–35).

Fellowship is religiously practiced by those who are devoted to Jesus. The church is designed for such. Those who do not take advantage of this great devotion are missing out on a great blessing God offers His children.

Know the Word of God. In *No Man Left Behind*, the authors write, "We have never known a single man whose life has changed in any significant way apart from the regular study of God's Word."[12]

How can a man wash his wife with the Word of God (Eph. 5:25–26) if he's weak about what the Word says?

Paul wrote to his pastoral protégé Timothy, "Be diligent to present yourself approved to God as a workman who does not need to be ashamed, accurately handling the word of truth" (2 Tim. 2:15). The Greek word translated as "accurately handling" literally means cutting or measuring something in a straight line.

Invest in God's kingdom. When God has your wallet, God has your heart.

Money is the god of the American dream and—sadly—many believers. Money exposes the heart of man. Test yourself. Do you give at least 10 percent of your household income to Christian causes you care about? Your answer is the answer to whether you have an idolatrous relationship with money.

By the way, your stuff isn't yours. It's on loan from the God who owns it all (Ps. 24). You're simply a steward of your resources—your money. The devout man obediently holds his wallet with an open hand, not a clenched fist. It's not about you. It's not about your stuff. It's about your God and what you do with His stuff.

Nurture people toward Jesus. Nowhere did Jesus ever say to make decisions for Him. Nowhere did He say to water down the gospel message and count converts. We have become a church of inviters instead of evangelists. Jesus said, "Go therefore and make disciples of all the nations, baptizing them in the name of the Father and the Son and the Holy Spirit, teaching them to observe all that I commanded you; and lo, I am with you always, even to the end of the age" (Matt. 28:19–20).

The devout teach the Bible, share their faith, train their children, read to their wives, and look for opportunities to discern a person's spiritual journey and move people closer to Jesus. Who are you actively involved in nurturing spiritually?

Give your life to the gospel's cause. The last of the seven religiously practiced disciplines of the full-capacity man is the grand finale, the climax, the overarching theme.

Years ago, the young custodian at my church asked if I would mentor him. He was gifted, intelligent, and had great potential except for a fatal flaw—he refused to clean the toilets. He was soon fired and found a job as a youth director of a small church. He lasted six months.

If a guy won't clean toilets, he isn't fit for ministry.

Conversely, I once had a spastic freshman and recent convert whose family did not attend church. Whenever the church doors opened, he was there, following the youth staff around and bombarding us with questions about God, church, and the Bible.

As my helper, he interrupted me in the middle of a game involving 150 screaming students. He wouldn't stop pulling my shirt trying to get my attention. Exasperated, I yelled, "Jacob, what do you want?"

"Well ... um ... someone dropped a dookie [pooped] on the boys' bathroom floor, but I already cleaned it up. It was gross. I just wanted to tell you."

Would you hire him as your youth pastor? Me too!

I've never met a man who was devoted to God who wasn't a tremendous servant in God's army. The two are inseparable.

DIAL IT IN
Small-Group Exercises

1. How are Romans 1:1 and 1 Peter 1:15–16 similar? Where have you devoted yourself, set your life apart, for God?

2. What is your understanding of the word *devout*? Where does religion play a positive role in devotion?

3. How is consistent attendance in a local fellowship critical for one's spiritual devotion (John 13:34–35; Heb. 10:23–25)?

4. What do John 13:15, Galatians 5:13, Philippians 2:3–4, and 1 Peter 4:10 teach about devotion?

5. Review the seven devout characteristics in the *walking* mnemonic device. Where do you have a slight limp?

6. Where are you the strongest?

ASSESSING YOUR CAPACITY

For each of the ten assessment statements, rank yourself accordingly:

> (5) Strongly agree
>
> (4) Agree
>
> (3) Neither agree nor disagree
>
> (2) Disagree
>
> (1) Strongly disagree

Add up your total score at the bottom, then add the overall score in the appendix on page 285.

1. I strive to find victory over sin. _____

My life looks different from the lives of those who do not follow Christ. _____

We should always preach the gospel and, if necessary, use words. _____

I confess my sins to God and others regularly. _____

I have regular prayer time. _____

The Bible says it. I believe it. I will obey it. _____

I attend church consistently. _____

My goal is to live a holy life, set apart for Jesus my Savior. _____

My life's passion is to be mastered by nothing but Christ alone. _____

I regularly fast as an expression of my commitment to Jesus. _____

TOTAL SCORE _____

THE RESPECTED MAN

The Greatest Gift a Man Can Be Given

Respect is a lot more important, and a lot greater, than popularity.

—Julius "Dr. J" Erving

I'm not concerned with your liking or disliking me....
All I ask is that you respect me as a human being.

—Jackie Robinson

R-E-S-P-E-C-T

Who can forget Aretha Franklin's 1960s hit song "Respect"? "R-E-S-P-E-C-T, Find out what it means to me."[1] The song earned Franklin two Grammy Awards and eventual induction into the Grammy Hall of Fame. In 2021, *Rolling Stone* magazine made it number one on their list of "The 500 Greatest Songs of All Time."[2]

But did you know that the song was written and performed by Otis Redding two years earlier, as a plea for respect from the woman he loved?[3]

Franklin flipped the script from a man pleading with his woman for a little respect to a demand for respect toward women.

I believe respect is the greatest gift a person, man or woman, can give a man.

KOSMIOS

I've always believed that when the Bible says it, that settles it. Unfortunately, we live in a world where "Christians" often shape the Word of God to fit their selfish desires, opinions, and philosophies. I always approach the Word with an open heart, asking God to let His Word saturate my heart and shape my life with truth. As we teach the principles of masculinity outlined in the Pastoral Epistles, it is critical that we accurately communicate the original intent, meaning, and context of every word or phrase.

The word translated "respectable" in 1 Timothy 3:2 in the New American Standard Bible is rendered in other versions as "well-behaved," "good behavior" (NKJV), or "well-thought-of" (MSG). To better understand its intended meaning, let's look at the Greek word *kosmios*.

Kosmios is described as "orderly, honest, respectful.... And is commonly used to describe a person who is a good citizen ... the person whose life is beautiful and in whose character all things are harmoniously integrated.... His inner control [is] being reflected in outward beauty."[4]

A few verses before 1 Timothy 3:2, Paul also used the word in his expectations of a woman's appearance in church: "Likewise, I want women to adorn themselves with proper clothing, **modestly** and discreetly, not with braided hair and gold or pearls or costly garments" (1 Tim. 2:9).

Kosmios is the root of the word *cosmetics*. It is a public display of the inner person. That makes sense. It is something we do and something people see in our lives. Essentially, it is bearing positive witness to our relationship with Jesus to a world that does not know Him.

The ancient Greek philosopher Plato said of the man who is *kosmios* that he "is the citizen who duly fulfills his place and order in the duties which are incumbent upon him as such."[5]

Cosmetics are meant to beautify. They bring out the best self. They cover flaws and accentuate a woman's best facial features. The man, however, who is *kosmios* lives in such a way as to make the gospel appealing rather than appalling. The godly man should be appealing to those in his circle of influence, not anonymous or appalling.

He is respected because of the exemplary way he lives. He is a man worthy of the greatest gift one man can give another: respect.

PAPA AND THE PRINCESS

"Papa, can I make your face?" I turned to see my precious four-year-old granddaughter, dressed as Princess Elsa from the movie *Frozen,* staring at me with her irresistible eyes.

After pondering my roles as a masculine thought leader, author, and communicator, I responded, "Naomi, do you know who I am? I lead an international men's ministry organization! Men look to me to help them understand what it means to be a man. I absolutely *will not* let you put makeup of any kind on my face. Now, go up to your room, and sit in time-out. I want you to think about what you just did!"

That's a lie.

I let her do it.

Then we took selfies and posted them on my social media platforms! By the time she was done, I looked more like a rodeo clown that had just been stomped by a bucking bronco than a prince! I looked appalling and not appealing at all, unless, of course, you like ogres! Watch out, Shrek, here I come! *Kosmios* should have made me look appealing, like Prince Charming instead of the toad before the kiss.

But it was worth it.

You may have lost all respect for me at this point, which is kind of ironic considering the title of this chapter. Hang on a little longer.

TAKE YOUR CAMO OFF

I'm a hunter and have been all my life. A couple of years ago, we started a family tradition. On my birthday, my sons (three by birth and one by choice) take me duck hunting. They choose the spot, throw the decoys, retrieve the ducks, and let me take the first shot. It is epic. Waterfowlers know that ducks fly best in the gray dawn of low-light conditions, but as the day progresses, especially on a clear day, ducks can see the brightness of a hunter's skin from a long distance.

When you hunt with us, face paint is required.

But when it is over, the face paint comes off. I want to stay married! At some point, the respected man takes his camo off. He removes his outer mask and reveals his authentic self through his actions over time.

Men who refuse to show their true selves are not respected by men who do. Others easily recognize them as posers, fakes, and charlatans. John Maxwell wrote, "When you don't have the strength within, you can't earn respect without."[6] The man who has strength within is not afraid to take his camo off. The authentic man shines as a beacon of hope for those living under the veneer of a hidden self.

I regularly meet with men from all backgrounds, careers, and demographics. Most meetings are life-giving. Some are rough. Really rough. Several years ago, I was compelled to meet with a Christian business owner who had grown his organization to dozens of employees. Early on, his faith was vibrant and outspoken. God blessed his business mightily. But it began to deteriorate as his faith began to waver.

He was often seen inebriated in public, had numerous questionable encounters with women, and often wrote off-color posts on social media. The net worth of his organization was rapidly declining, and his employees were resigning at an alarming rate. His business was being damaged by his poor witness.

He lost the respect of his subordinates, evidenced by his company's high turnover rates. He refused to take the camo off. Something was broken, but his bravado would not allow him to admit it. After a long and awkward discussion about his life and declining witness, he smirked and offered the last words I ever heard from him: "I just don't understand why you believe in all this authentic stuff."

Sometime later, sexual misconduct allegations compelled him to resign his position and leave town with his tail between his legs. His company has yet to recover.

Respect can take decades to earn but be lost in seconds. Respect is the greatest gift that can be given to a man, but once it is lost, it is lost. Most men would rather have respect from their wives than love. I bet most men would rather have respect than sex, knowing that if one has the former, he will receive an abundance of the latter.

For a man to enhance the world around him, like cosmetics enhance a woman's beauty, he must take his mask off first.

Take the camo off. Earn the great gift of respect.

MORE THAN SEX?

I used to wonder why I cared more about Shanna respecting me than loving me until I read Emerson Eggerichs's *Love and Respect*, a monumental book on marriage, which has sold over two million copies. In our podcast interview, Eggerichs shared how God gave him an epiphany while studying the household codes of Ephesians 5:25–33.

> Husbands, **love your wives**, just as Christ also loved the church and gave Himself up for her, so that He might sanctify her, having cleansed her by the washing of water with the word, that He might present to Himself the church in all her glory, having no spot or wrinkle or any such thing; but that she would be holy and blameless. So husbands ought also to **love their own wives** as their own bodies. He who **loves his own wife** loves himself; for no one ever hated his own flesh, but nourishes and cherishes it, just as Christ also does the church, because we are members of His body. For this reason a man shall leave his father and mother and shall be joined to his wife, and the two shall become one flesh. This mystery is great; but I am speaking with reference to Christ and the church. Nevertheless, each individual among you also is to **love his own wife** even

as himself, and the wife must see to it that she **respects her husband**.

Eggerichs said he realized that in the longest passage on marriage in the New Testament, women are never commanded to love their husbands, but on *four separate* occasions (vv. 25, 28a, 28b, 33), men are told to love their wives. The only thing women are told is to respect their husbands (v. 33)!

Why?

Because love is the default for women. They naturally love. They are made for it. They are built for it. It comes easy. But respect is not, which is why God invites them into that space. It is not natural. It is not their default. God, in His ingenuity, asks wives to do what doesn't come naturally—to do that which will take great discipline and focus to master. He asks them to respect their husbands.

In the same way, four times God asks the men to do what doesn't come naturally to them—to love. I'll let you guess why God told men to love their wives four times and made only one mention of wives respecting their husbands! Sometimes we need a little repetition.

Why does God say this to women? Because it is the greatest gift, even greater than sex, that a wife can give her husband. I know men who aren't satisfied sexually by their wives but remain faithful anyway. Why? Because their wives respect them. I know other men (far more) who had great sex lives but ran away with the secretary because she gave him what he desperately needed: respect. The adultery came later.

Bill Perkins was right when he wrote, "Men place respect at the top of their hierarchy of needs."[7] I wish more wives understood this deep-seated need men have. But men know it. If you are not a man with *kosmios*, you will struggle to impact those around you for Jesus. Earlier in the book, I alluded to how I lost the respect of a handful of men, and a decade later, they still struggle to look me in the eye. Respect is hard-earned but easily tossed into the trash. When a man gives you his respect, he gives you the keys to his life. When you lose that respect, he grabs his keys and kicks you out of the house.

If you don't have respect, little else matters. Respect is the greatest gift one man can give another.

COSMETICS AND THE LOCAL WAITRESS

My job requires regularly meeting with people over coffee or a meal. I know, it sucks. A while back, something started to bother me. I finally realized the solution to my heartburn.

If you met me, you would say, "He's a nice guy." The barista smiles when I walk into the coffee shop and calls me by name, "Norm, what's going on?"

"It's a dog-eat-dog world, and I'm wearing Milk-Bone underwear!"

Forgive the line from the '80s show *Cheers*. I couldn't help myself. Anyway, I'm friendly, I'm kind, and I'm a good tipper. It bothered my soul that I might be remembered as a nice guy and good tipper while many of my unsaved tippees are on AC/DC's "Highway to Hell," and I am smiling all the way. So, I decided to stop being nice. I opted for *kosmios* instead. Now, when I'm eating out, I will often learn the server's name. When they bring the meal out, I stop them and, addressing them by name, I say, "I pray for my meals, and I am about to pray for you. Is there anything specific I can pray about for you?"

At that point, the floodgates open. One day, my server was Nate, a young man with long hair and a scraggly beard. To say he was rough-looking would be an understatement, and I was initially intimidated to ask him. But he erupted with what his heart was holding in, "Yes! Please! I have PTSD from the military and am struggling right now."

At that moment we created a bond. I pray for Nate whenever I think of him. I'm praying for him now. I earned his respect that day. At my local restaurants, I am respected as a good tipper and a man of God. I am not nice to servers anymore, but I am *kosmios*. I long to earn the greatest gift a man can be given: respect.

DIAL IT IN
Small-Group Exercises

1. Why is being respected so important to your masculinity?

2. Compare the word *kosmios* used in 1 Timothy 2:9 and 3:2. How would you define the word if you were translating these verses from Greek to English?

3. Can you think of anyone who struggles to look you in the eye because something you did or said caused them to lose respect for you?

4. Read Matthew 22:38–39. What kind of neighbor are you—good, bad, or ugly—and why? Do you have any neighbors that may be hindered from coming to Christ because of your lack of *kosmios*?

5. Read Matthew 5:13–16. Jesus said we are to be the "salt of the earth" and the "light of the world." Share at least one habit you've formed to strategically impact those around you.

6. Read Ephesians 5:25–33. How does your love for your wife (or lack thereof) and her respect for you (or lack thereof) impact your marriage?

7. Wives are commanded to respect their husbands based on their title of "husband," and that's on them. But what can you start doing differently to earn the respect of your bride?

ASSESSING YOUR CAPACITY

For each of the ten assessment statements, rank yourself accordingly:

(5) Strongly agree

(4) Agree

(3) Neither agree nor disagree

(2) Disagree

(1) Strongly disagree

Add up your total score at the bottom, then add the overall score in the appendix on page 286.

1. I have been told that I am a role model. _____

I am known as a man of my word. _____

I try to engage with my unbelieving friends. _____

I am known as a man who pays my bills on time. _____

I am regularly asked for advice. _____

I know my nearby neighbors by name. _____

I regularly volunteer in my community. _____

I relate well to Jesus calling His followers "salt" and
"light." _____

I believe in establishing deep roots in my community. _____

My neighbors would say I am a good neighbor. _____

TOTAL SCORE _____

THE SACRIFICIAL MAN

Think of Yourself Less

For the overseer must ... not [be] self-willed.

—Titus 1:7

Humility is not thinking less of yourself;
it is thinking of yourself less.

—Rick Warren, *The Purpose Driven Life*

HACKSAW RIDGE

Desmond Doss never fired a rifle in combat. He never held one except for using it as a splint for his shattered arm after being shot off a makeshift stretcher. As a devout follower of Jesus and conscientious objector, he served as a combat medic during World War II. He was awarded the Bronze Star Medal twice for his heroic achievements and meritorious service in combat.

He is famously known as the only conscientious objector to receive the Medal of Honor during the war. He demonstrated unusual bravery in the Battle of Okinawa after saving the lives of seventy-five men, as portrayed in the 2016 Oscar-winning film *Hacksaw Ridge*.

In the battle, Doss's combat unit was tasked with using rope ladders to climb a four-hundred-foot cliff and secure the Maeda Escarpment, also known as Hacksaw Ridge.

At the beginning of the fight and during the next morning, with heavy losses on both sides, the Japanese launched a massive counterattack and drove the Americans off the escarpment. Remaining on the ridge, Doss heard wounded soldiers crying for help and returned to save them, carrying the wounded to the cliff's edge and lowering them down by rope, each time praying, "Please, Lord, help me get one more."[1]

Here is an excerpt from the citation for Doss's Medal of Honor:

> He was a company aid man when the 1st Battalion assaulted a jagged escarpment 400 feet high. As our troops gained the summit, a heavy concentration of artillery, mortar and machinegun fire crashed into them, inflicting approximately 75 casualties and driving the others back. Private First Class Doss refused to seek cover and remained in the fire-swept area with the many stricken, carrying them one by one to the edge of the escarpment and there lowering them on a rope-supported litter down the face of a cliff to friendly hands. On 2 May, he exposed himself to heavy rifle and mortar fire in rescuing a wounded man 200 yards forward of the lines on the same escarpment;

and two days later he treated four men who had been cut down while assaulting a strongly defended cave, advancing through a shower of grenades to within eight yards of enemy forces in a cave's mouth, where he dressed his comrades' wounds before making four separate trips under fire to evacuate them to safety. On 5 May, he unhesitatingly braved enemy shelling and small-arms fire to assist an artillery officer. He applied bandages, moved his patient to a spot that offered protection from small-arms fire and, while artillery and mortar shells fell close by, painstakingly administered plasma. Later that day, when an American was severely wounded by fire from a cave, Private First Class Doss crawled to him where he had fallen 25 feet from the enemy position, rendered aid, and carried him 100 yards to safety while continually exposed to enemy fire. On 21 May, in a night attack on high ground near Shuri, he remained in exposed territory while the rest of his company took cover, fearlessly risking the chance that he would be mistaken for an infiltrating Japanese and giving aid to the injured until he was himself seriously wounded in the legs by the explosion of a grenade. Rather than call another aid man from cover, he cared for his injuries and waited five hours before litter bearers reached him and started carrying him to cover. The trio was caught in an enemy tank attack and Private First Class Doss, seeing a more critically wounded man nearby, crawled off the litter and directed the bearers to give their first attention to the other man. Awaiting the litter bearers' return, he was again struck, this time suffering a compound fracture of one arm. With magnificent fortitude he bound a rifle stock to his shattered arm as a splint and then crawled 300 yards over rough terrain to the aid station. Through his outstanding bravery and unflinching determination in the face of desperately dangerous conditions Private First Class Doss saved the lives of many soldiers. His name became a symbol throughout the 77th Infantry Division for outstanding gallantry far above and beyond the call of duty.[2]

"Please, Lord, help me get one more."

Such heroism is found only in the man who is prepared to sacrifice his life for others. Doss's actions were inspired by the ultimate sacrifice of Jesus, who said, "Greater love has no one than this, that one lay down his life for his friends" (John 15:13). The sacrificial man embraces the truth of Rick Warren's words, "It's not about you."[3] It's about Jesus, bringing glory to Him and sacrificing oneself for the benefit of others. Dialed in men willingly and joyfully sacrifice themselves for others.

It is one thing to serve others through praying for them, giving financially, or volunteering, and I'm not discounting those vital components of our faith. But sacrifice is different, because of the cost involved. If it doesn't hurt deeply, if it doesn't cause you to stop, pause, and pray, then it probably isn't sacrificing. When was the last time you took a great risk for God that cost you—personally—more than you could have ever imagined? Men who are dialed in learn to sacrifice not because they think less of themselves, but because they think of themselves less. The sacrificial man is the cream that rises to the top.

TITANIC COMPARISONS

People often confuse serving (see chapter 2) with sacrifice, because both often encompass an event. For example, Doss served the wounded men of his battalion, thereby blessing them with his great act of service.

But he served them at the risk of his own life. He *sacrificed his rights* to serve the wounded men on the Maeda Escarpment.

So, how is serving different from sacrifice? Glad you asked.

Sacrifice is the act of surrendering something of high value, such as our lives, our rights, or our freedom, for the sake of others. It requires an inward decision to potentially suffer for the benefit of others. In contrast, service is using our time, talents, or treasures to enrich the lives of others. This is what Jesus meant when He said, "Truly, truly, I say to you, unless a grain of wheat falls into the earth and dies, it remains alone; but if it dies, it bears much fruit. He who loves his life loses it, and he who hates his life in this world will keep it to life eternal" (John 12:24–25).

The man who willingly dies to himself for Christ lays down his life for others. Galatians 2:20 is his war cry: "I have been crucified with Christ; and it is no longer I who live, but Christ lives in me; and the life which I now live in the flesh I live by faith in the Son of God, who loved me and gave Himself up for me."

The sacrificial man is a dead man walking, not because he thinks less of himself, but because he thinks of himself less.

Take the film *Titanic* and its **fictional** account of the maiden voyage of the Titanic, during which 1,514 tragically died—fictional because the lead female character is engaged to a cowardly millionaire who steals a place on a lifeboat, ultimately costing a woman or child their life. What the movie purposely neglects are the brave men who willingly sacrificed their lives for women and children. Of the more than 2,200 people aboard the Titanic that infamous night, only 706 survived—1,360 of those who died were men!

Only 157 women and children perished, many because they were trapped in the lower decks.[4]

Why?

Men went down with the ship to sacrifice their lives for others. These brave men never flinched. They never thought twice about their sacrifice. Insurmountable numbers of men throughout history have sacrificed themselves for the safety, rights, and freedom of others.

It is true in history, it is true today, and it will always be true. Watch the news. When catastrophe strikes, it is men who come to the rescue.

Why? Because God has wired men, strong men, to sacrifice themselves for the greater good. When the world needs someone to think of themselves less, at the risk of their own lives, it is almost always a man. And never a male.

Now let's look at the opposite of self-sacrifice that Paul spoke against in Titus 1:7 when he wrote, "For the overseer must ... not [be] self-willed."

MY WAY OR THE HIGHWAY

The word Paul used to describe the self-willed man is the compound Greek word *authades*, which comes from *autos*, meaning "self," and *hedomai*, meaning "take one's pleasure." It is where we get the word *hedonist*. *Authades*, then, means "self-pleasing, self-willed, arrogant, or overbearing."[5]

This is an ugly picture of the man who is dominated by self-interest, is inconsiderate of others, and arrogantly asserts his own will.[6] *Authades* is the opposite of gentleness, which we will discuss in chapter 19. The self-willed man is like a *self-walled* man—he builds a world around himself. He lives his dream to the neglect of others. He is obsessed with his personal gain, pleasure, and agenda at the expense of others. In sports, we call this person a prima donna. He's not a team player because he doesn't care about anyone but himself, his accolades, and personal recognition.

Commenting on Paul's admonition against this self-willed arrogance, Matthew Henry wrote,

> The prohibition is to a large extent, excluding self-opinion, or overweening conceit of parts and abilities, and abounding in one's sense—self-love, and self-seeking, making self the center of all—also self-confidence and trust, and self-pleasing, little regarding or setting by others—being proud, stubborn, forward, inflexible, set on one's own will and way.[7]

Is this what you aspire to? I hope not. This guy couldn't care less about the win-win. All he cares about is a win for himself at any cost. He loathes sacrifice. He despises it. He is a self-serving hedonist at his core. He lives by the creed "It's my way or the highway," expecting others to pay homage to his brilliant understanding. He disregards the interests of others to please himself. He is the archnemesis of the sacrificial man.

Do you know how I know this? It takes one to know one. I *was* this man. But no more. Jesus changed me.

I vividly remember my high school senior awards night, before I started my journey with Christ. The student body and class presidents, two of my best friends, were tasked with giving awards to certain class-mates. I proudly stood up as they announced my title, "Jim Ramos, most likely to be on the cover of Sports Illustrated ..."

I puffed my chest out and sauntered to the podium. When I was halfway to the stage they shouted in unison, "... and tell you about it!"

It was a wake-up call I've never forgotten.

Archbishop of Dublin, Richard Trench described the *authades* man: "He obstinately maintains his own opinion, or asserts his rights, while he is reckless of the rights, opinions, and interests of others."[8] Syrian philoso-pher Philodemus described his character as being "made up of equal parts of conceit, arrogance, and contemptuousness. His conceit made him think too highly of himself; his contemptuousness made him think too meanly of others; and his arrogance made him act on his restimate of humself and others."[9] The self-willed man has a massive character flaw that can only be solved through imitating Jesus' sacrifice and thinking of himself less.

The *authades* man is conceited. He is excessively proud of himself, and he is willing to tell you about it. He sucks the air out of a room when he enters. He dominates conversations. He never asks about others because they don't matter in his universe, where everything revolves around him.

He is arrogant. He has an exaggerated sense of his importance and abilities. Exaggerated in the sense that his opinions of himself are not necessarily true, but they are true to him. We see a form of this in the helicopter mom or bulldozer dad who believes their kid is a super athlete or genius when they are often just a big fish in a tiny pond.

He is contemptuous. He shows scorn, contempt, and ridicule for anyone who may threaten his position, status, or opinion of himself. All threats must be eliminated. His view of competition is demented because winning isn't the primary goal. Eliminating his competition is.

The only sacrifice he is willing to make is for—you guessed it—himself. He thinks too much of himself, whereas his nemesis, the sacrificial man, thinks of himself less.

THE MURPH

The Murph is possibly the most popular workout on the planet. I've heard it mentioned in movies and on television and by people who know nothing about CrossFit. A Hero WOD (workout of the day), the Murph is completed every year on Memorial Day by CrossFitters, Navy SEALs, and anyone willing to experience a great challenge.

I experienced the Murph firsthand.

It sucked. The workout is simple: a one-mile "buy-in" run, followed by one hundred pull-ups, two hundred push-ups, three hundred body squats, and another one-mile run. It took over an hour to complete and, in the process, ripped a callous off my hand on my ninety-fifth pull-up. I still remember staring at that bleeding crater on my palm thinking, *Now what!*

It was one of the favorite workouts of Lieutenant Michael P. Murphy. His sacrifice is depicted in the 2013 film *Lone Survivor.* He and the others on his SEAL team, except for Marcus Luttrell, were killed during a reconnaissance mission to find a key Taliban leader in Afghanistan when the team came under fire from a much larger enemy force. Murphy knowingly left his position of cover to get a clear signal to communicate with his headquarters. He died fighting for that vulnerable position. He sacrificed his life for his brothers, epitomizing the truly sacrificial man.

He thought of himself less.

DIAL IT IN
Small-Group Exercises

1. Share a story about a time you made a great sacrifice for someone you loved. Besides the time you spend at work, how do you sacrifice yourself for those you love?

2. In Titus 1:7, Paul used the word *authades* to describe what a man should **not** be. Depending on the Bible version, the word can be translated as "self-willed" (KJV, NASB, NKJV), "overbearing" (NIV), or "arrogant" (ESV, HCSB, NLT). Which of these do you resonate with, and why?

3. Besides Titus 1:7, the only other time *authades* is mentioned in the New Testament is in 2 Peter 2:10–11. How do you interpret "self-willed" in the context of these two passages?

4. What did Paul mean by "holy sacrifice" as a "spiritual service of worship" in Romans 12:1?

5. How is love a motivator for sacrifice (John 10:10–11; 15:13)?

6. How is the death of self through Christian surrender critical for the sacrificial man (John 12:24–25; Gal. 2:20; 6:14)?

7. What do Ephesians 5:1–2, Hebrews 13:15–16, and 1 Peter 2:5 teach about Christian sacrifice?

ASSESSING YOUR CAPACITY

For each of the ten assessment statements, rank yourself accordingly:

(5) Strongly agree

(4) Agree

(3) Neither agree nor disagree

(2) Disagree

(1) Strongly disagree

Add up your total score at the bottom, then add the overall score in the appendix on page 287.

1. I think of others more than I think of myself. _____

   I am willing to listen and adjust if someone's idea is better than mine. _____

   My goal is to encourage people in every interaction. _____

   Laying your life down for another is the highest of callings. _____

   When I am wrong, I readily admit it. _____

   I regularly ask about a person's story even if I never get to share mine. _____

   I am not threatened by the great achievements of others. _____

   We must all learn to sacrifice ourselves for the greater good. _____

   I am inspired by watching men sacrifice their lives for a great cause. _____

   I am content not being recognized for my service. _____

   TOTAL SCORE _____

THE LEADER

Do Something, Anything—Just Lead

An overseer, then ... must be one who manages his own household well, keeping his children under control with all dignity (but if a man does not know how to manage his own household, how will he take care of the church of God?).

—1 Timothy 3:2, 4–5

Appoint elders in every city as I directed you, namely, if any man is above reproach, the husband of one wife, having children who believe.

—Titus 1:5–6

POSITION DOUBTFUL

Amelia Mary Earhart was an aviation pioneer and author who was instrumental in the formation of the Ninety-Nines, an organization for female pilots. In 1928, she became the first female passenger to cross the

Atlantic by airplane, giving her celebrity status. In 1932, she became the first woman to fly solo across the Atlantic Ocean. Then July 2, 1937, she set out with Frederick Noonan as her navigator to be the first person to fly around the world at the equator. But somewhere in the western Pacific near New Guinea, she lost her bearings. Her last radio message was, "Position doubtful."[1]

A massive search found nothing but the ocean, and Earhart was officially declared dead in 1939.

What about her navigator, Frederick Noonan? Whatever happened to him? I heard that he lived to a ripe old age and died in peace with his family by his side somewhere on the Fiji islands.

I just made that up. He was lost at sea and pronounced dead with Earhart. You see, when the captain loses his or her bearings, so does the crew.

Earhart's tragic loss of position reminds me of the myriads of men who are lost somewhere within the child-raising years. The father's intentions are admirable. His motives are pure. He wakes up and grinds it out daily, but somewhere along the way, he loses his bearing. He forgets himself. Forgets who he is. Forgets where he is. He gets tragically lost in his own story.

His status is "position doubtful." Sadly, his crew gets lost along the way as well.

LeRoy Eims wrote, "A leader is one who sees more than others see, who sees farther than others see, and who sees before others see."[2] His default setting is the Word of God, so even when his position is temporarily doubtful, he continues to lead the way in truth.

Spiritual leadership is quite simple. No matter where you are in your spiritual journey or how old your children may be, my advice is the same—do something. Anything. Just lead. I hesitate to tell men what I do or did for fear that it might discourage them from doing something. When you do receive spiritual leadership advice, keep in mind that most of the time, the people offering it are vocational Christians and are often exaggerating the truth to affirm their expertise.

Do something. Anything. Just lead.

THAT ONE WORD

It is mind-boggling how many men are caught off guard by one word: spiritual. That one word has stopped men in their tracks. That one word has caused some of the most successful leaders I know to scratch their heads in dismay. That one word has paralyzed some of the most action-oriented leaders I know.

The word *spiritual* in the phrase "spiritual leadership" has led to much confusion, and it's been that way for two millennia. Look at the Pastoral Epistles, for example. This chapter is distinct because even though the term *spiritual leader* is never mentioned in Scripture, Paul spent more time in the Pastoral Epistles describing household leadership than any of the other nineteen qualities, most of which are one-word descriptions.

When we think of the biblical quality of leadership, it is important to note that Paul was addressing more than a man's marriage and children, although those are primary components. I remember when we moved to Oregon how hard it was for my sons, who were four, six, and eight years old, to adjust to life without their grandparents, their friends, and the church they were used to. A couple of months after I was hired, our pastor called me into his office because our youngest son, Colton, was acting out in Sunday school. He said something memorable to me: "You will never be fired because of your children but how you respond to them."

I took that to heart. Let's look at the three components of leadership Paul mapped out in 1 Timothy 3:4–5 and Titus 1:6, so when in doubt, you will do something. Anything. Just lead.

"MANAGES HIS OWN HOUSEHOLD WELL" (1 TIMOTHY 3:4)

It is important to understand that the ancient "household" looked different from what it does today. It was common to have multiple generations, servants, and business associates living in the same household. The word for "manages" Paul used in 1 Timothy 3:4 is the Greek *proistemi,* meaning "to rule, superintend, or preside over." A man's managerial responsibilities at the time would have extended to all those under his roof, including his adult children and parents.[3]

This is important since children are living at home longer than they were fifty years ago. Each of our sons was able to buy a home a couple of years after graduating from college, in part because we invited them back into our home for up to a year after graduating from college to save money and gain financial traction. But they lived by our house rules under my authority during that time.

No questions asked. Our home. Our rules. Follow them or leave.

If *proistemi* means to preside and provide, the following are some of the critical items a spiritual leader presides over and provides. Here is a word picture I use to describe *proistemi* and what it looks like to manage one's household. Like a roof, he **presides over** his household, shielding those in his house from outside forces that could harm them. Thus, he **protects** them. Like the barriers surrounding the home structure, he is an impenetrable wall, guarding the hearts of those under his care. He **provides** for their primary needs of food, water, and shelter.

Like the rooms in a house, his people have a secure place under his leadership.

Proistemi. He presides over (the roof). He protects (the wall). He provides (the rooms). Below are some practical examples of *proistemi* in the real world.

Food, water, and shelter. As a wilderness hunter, I learned to survive in the wilderness for weeks with just a backpack. But I will be malnourished, dirty, sleep-deprived, and generally uncomfortable the whole time. A good leader provides an adequate environment for his family to physically thrive, which leads to the next point.

Fitness. Gluttony is an acceptable sin in the church. In our opulent modern culture, it is more important than ever that a spiritual leader manages the health and diet of his household. Don't be that man whose position is doubtful when it comes to navigating your family toward health and longevity.

Family. Shanna and I invest in our marriage constantly—religiously having date nights when the boys were young, taking one full day off to rest, and using all my allotted vacation time every year. As my sons were growing up, I often told them I loved them very much—so often, in fact, that it became boring for them to hear. I also made it crystal clear that I loved their mother more. I'm so glad we invested in our marriage in those ways. We are reaping the rewards of a great marriage today.

Faith. The dialed in man models three things religiously: living biblically, serving consistently, and practicing spiritual disciplines habitually. My sons once questioned if our mandate to attend church was because I worked at a church. My answer was simple, "Yes, but even if I didn't work at a church, you would have been required to go, because that is what devoted followers of Jesus do."

Finances. Presiding over a household requires good financial management, which to me means four things: tithing, paying bills on time, managing debt (preferably having none), and planning for the future. About finances, John MacArthur wrote, "He [the spiritual leader] must be a good steward of his house and his finances—all people and resources over which he has responsibility. Someone, for example, who managed his family well, but mismanaged his money and possessions, would be disqualified."[4]

Friendships. It is your job to manage the relationships your children have while they are in your home. The Bible is clear in saying, "Do not be deceived: 'Bad company corrupts good morals'" (1 Cor. 15:33). Knowing this truth, my wife and I were strategic in a few critical areas. We built a trusted and effective network with the parents of our kids' friends. We approved all friendships before they got too deeply involved (especially with girls), and we didn't give our sons large windows of free time, which bleeds into our next category.

Fun. As adults, our sons have commented on how much leeway we gave them as they neared high school graduation. We let their choices limit or expand their horizons. We implemented boundaries when they were young so they would earn our trust as they matured. By creating boundaries, I mean we kept them too busy to make (too many) poor choices.

Freedom. My sons are not perfect because their parents are not perfect. There are several things I'd do differently if I had the chance. We weren't perfect, but we were good enough to raise three free sons. It is vital to raise children who become adults who are free from the bondage of food, sex, booze, and drugs. Frederick Douglass is credited as saying, "It is easier to build strong children than to repair broken men [and women]." Manage any sin in your camp (Josh. 7:1–17). Keep your finger on the pulse.

"KEEPING HIS CHILDREN UNDER CONTROL WITH ALL DIGNITY" (1 TIMOTHY 3:4)

There are four words for "child" in the Greek language: *nepios* (infant), *paidion* (toddler to pre-teen), *teknon* (physically mature yet emotionally immature teenager), and *huios* (fully formed adult). *Teknon*, which describes a preteen to teenager or a child living in willing dependence, is the word used in both 1 Timothy 3:4 and Titus 1:6, describing a physically fully formed but mentally immature person. The word includes children who have chosen to live within the physical walls under the spiritual mantle of their parents.

The thirty-second president of the United States, Franklin D. Roosevelt, was right when he said, "We cannot always build the future for our youth, but we can build our youth for the future."[5] Christian parents are biblically accountable for the actions of their children from infancy through their teen years. Another way of putting it is that you are responsible for your children while they are under your roof.

I recently wondered about some Christian parents who allowed their adult child to live in their home with free room and board, paid their cell phone bill and car insurance, and yet allowed them to openly smoke marijuana in their home, saying it was the child's choice. These parents deferred their authority to their child, which in my opinion is a strike against the father's leadership because he chose to do nothing.

Do something. Anything. Just lead.

"HAVING CHILDREN WHO BELIEVE" (TITUS 1:6)

Someone once said, "Success is being respected the most by those who know me the best." My direct family includes those who see me most when my guard is down and know me better than anyone else. Be less concerned about your kids listening to you, and more worried that they are watching your every move!

Founder of Focus on the Family, James Dobson, rightly observed that "children are not casual guests in our home. They have been loaned to us temporarily for the purpose of loving them and instilling a foundation of values on which their future lives will be built."[6]

Jesus indicated that the Enemy follows a dire progression: "The thief comes only to steal and kill and destroy" (John 10:10).

It was common practice for ancient conquering kings to not only kill the conquered king but destroy his lineage by murdering all his bloodline. Did you know that "your adversary, the devil, prowls around like a roaring lion" looking for the opportunity to destroy your godly legacy (1 Pet. 5:8)? If you are saved, Satan is hell-bent on you being the last one in your bloodline to enter heaven! The stakes are high.

Again, Paul used the word *teknon* to describe "children who believe" (Titus 1:6).

We led each of our sons to Jesus on their half birthdays when they turned five-and-a-half years old and still celebrate those days as a reminder of the day they came to Jesus. We wanted our sons to have memorable baptisms, so we baptized each in a private ceremony when they entered their teen years: James on Maui (Hawaii), Darby in Shasta Lake (Northern California), and Colton in Caye Caulker (Belize). We remind them of those forever moments often.

The dialed in spiritual leader lives by Joshua 24:15, "As for me and my house, we will serve the LORD."

DIAL IT IN
Small-Group Exercises

1. Think about the statement: "Do something. Anything. Just lead." Where can you improve as a spiritual leader? What one thing can you do today?

2. Which of the three areas mentioned in 1 Timothy 3:2, 4–5 and Titus 1:6 can you improve upon the most: (1) managing your own household well, (2) keeping your children under control with all dignity, or (3) having children who believe?

3. What fathering advice can you see from the following verses: Proverbs 22:6, 1 Corinthians 15:33, Ephesians 6:4, and 1 Thessalonians 2:10–11?

4. The Greek *proistemi* means "to preside and provide." Which of the following items stands out the most for your situation and why: food, water, shelter, fitness and health, family, faith, finances, friendships, fun, or freedom?

5. Review the four Greek words for "child": *nepios*, *paidion*, *teknon*, and *huios*. Based on these words and definitions, where would you spiritually place each of your children? Also, consider where you would place your wife. Does any need specific prayer today?

ASSESSING YOUR CAPACITY

For each of the ten assessment statements, rank yourself accordingly:

(5) Strongly agree

(4) Agree

(3) Neither agree nor disagree

(2) Disagree

(1) Strongly disagree

Add up your total score at the bottom, then add the overall score in the appendix on page 288.

1. I lead by Joshua 24:15, "As for me and my house, we will serve the LORD."   _____

My wife trusts my spiritual leadership.   _____

We regularly pray over meals at least once a day as a family.   _____

My children attend at least one Christian gathering a week.   _____

Biblical obedience is required in our home.   _____

My children are not perfect, but they are well-adjusted and follow Jesus.   _____

I use godly wisdom to discipline my children.   _____

My children have a good reputation in our community.   _____

My wife gladly attends church with me.   _____

My children obey my wife and me and treat us with respect.   _____

TOTAL SCORE   _____

THE TEACHER

Cut It Straight

The Lord's bond-servant must not be quarrelsome, but be kind to all, able to teach, patient when wronged.

—2 Timothy 2:24

Be diligent to present yourself approved to God as a workman who does not need to be ashamed, accurately handling the word of truth.

—2 Timothy 2:15

CUT IT STRAIGHT

There are many meals I have eaten and forgotten about, but there is one lunch I clearly remember. Kim, whom I had never met before, was our server. As she delivered our meals, I leaned back and quietly shared that we pray for our meals and were going to pray for her, and I asked if she had anything on her heart we could pray for.

She excitedly said, "Yes! Pray for my faith!"

Kim then stood reverently behind me, bowed her head, closed her eyes, and waited for her prayer. I quickly prayed for our food and her faith. Immediately she launched into her story of how a few months earlier she had come to Christ out of a cult when she found a Gideons' Bible in a hotel drawer. She compared that Bible to the "Bible" her church used and realized there were some massive discrepancies between the two versions that no one in her cult church was willing to discuss.

Subsequently, she came to Christ, was excommunicated from the cult, and, several months later, led her husband to Christ! Since both of their families were part of the cult, they both had been cut off from their families, which is why she needed prayer. This situation reminded me of Paul's warning to Timothy: "Be diligent to present yourself approved to God as a workman who does not need to be ashamed, accurately handling the word of truth" (2 Tim. 2:15). The Greek word translated "accurately handling" means cutting something straight, like a man swinging an axe or sawing through a piece of wood in a straight line.

Essentially Paul was telling Timothy to cut the Word straight, accurately, never tilting one way or the other.

The dialed in man recognizes the tremendous power of the Word of God and is careful to wield this "sword of the Spirit" with the greatest of care (Eph. 6:17). Ronald Reagan is credited with saying, "Within the covers of the Bible are the answers for all the problems men face." Scripture has the power to change lives because "the word of God is living and active and sharper than any two-edged sword, and piercing as far as the division of soul and spirit, of both joints and marrow, and able to judge the thoughts and intentions of the heart" (Heb. 4:12).

Dialed in men learn to cut it straight.

I agree with genius Isaac Newton, whose views of the Bible's power have been summarized this way: "I have a fundamental belief in the Bible as the Word of God, written by those who were inspired. I study the Bible daily."

If you are reading this, you most likely agree with Newton's comment. The goal of this chapter is to unpack what it means for the dialed in man to live as if he believes Scripture is the truth of God.

UNIQUE

This chapter is unique from the other nineteen on this point: being able to teach is the *only* quality that relates specifically to a man's talent and function. First Timothy, 2 Timothy, and Titus are called the Pastoral Epistles because they address the character and function of spiritual leaders, which should be the goal of every Christian man.

In context, being able to teach is one talent that sets the elder or overseer apart from deacons. Some men simply are not gifted teachers. I know men who understand the Bible better than I do and have more verses memorized than I do but are unable to effectively engage, teach, or explain the Scriptures. But having the ability to teach is much more than sermon delivery or public speaking. We have grossly misunderstood what being able to teach means in the context of spiritual leaders and men who are dialed in.

Cutting the Word of God straight happens more on Monday through Saturday than in church on Sundays.

STAND UP, SPEAK UP, SIT DOWN, SHUT UP

I dropped every college course that required public speaking, so you can imagine my horror when God used a verse from the Bible to call me to preach: "You are the most excellent of men and your lips have been anointed with grace, since God has blessed you forever" (Ps. 45:2NIV).[1] I begrudgingly said yes. As God slowly equipped my call, a respected older pastor taught me a wise principle. He said, "Whenever you speak, stand up to be seen, speak up to be heard, sit down to be appreciated, and shut up to glorify God."

I also learned the humbling truth that someone will always compliment your teaching. Someone will always be there to criticize it too. Only my family will tell me the brutal truth! So, stand up, speak up, sit down, and shut up.

I was with a good friend recently who was sharing about the eldership of his church and how one of the elders was not biblically qualified because he did not have the mystical ability to teach. Though I admired my friend's zeal, I disagreed with his interpretation.

Being able to teach is much more than preaching in a church. It is offering biblical counsel. It is leading a Bible study. It is admonishing others on social media. It is writing a blog about what the Bible teaches. It is posting a video about the truths of God. According to William Barclay, "The finest and most effective teaching is done not by speaking but by being. Even those with no gift of words can teach, by living in such a way that in them others see the reflection of the Master."[2]

John MacArthur made a great observation about being able to teach that plays perfectly to my point: "Some may wonder why Paul includes this qualification in the midst of a list of moral qualities. He does so because effective teaching is woven into the moral character of the teacher. What a man is cannot be divorced from what he says."[3]

Did you catch that? What and how you teach is an overflow of the real you. This sounds a lot like what someone else once said: "For the mouth speaks out of that which fills the heart. The good man brings out of his good treasure what is good; and the evil man brings out of his evil treasure what is evil" (Matt. 12:34–35).

Look at 1 Timothy 3:2–4 in context and notice how the ability to teach is sandwiched between *six* character qualities on either side:

> An overseer, then, must be above reproach, the husband of one wife, temperate, prudent, respectable, hospitable, **able to teach,** not addicted to wine or pugnacious, but gentle, peaceable, free from the love of money. He must be one who manages his own household well, keeping his children under control with all dignity.

Gene Getz rightly observed that this was not a coincidence:

> Clearly, to be *able to teach* means that we must learn how to communicate with others in a nonthreatening, non-defensive manner. We are to avoid arguments by being sensitive to people who are confused or even obstinate.... In short, a man who is able to teach is a person who is not in bondage to himself. Rather, his true identity in Jesus Christ has enabled him to be in control of his mind and emotions.[4]

We live in a time when faith in Christ is under fire. In fact, throughout history, the underlying message of Christianity has been unpopular. There is one God. One Messiah. One way to heaven. Only those who

believe in Jesus will be with God for eternity in heaven. Our message has
been and always will be opposed by the majority.

The gospel must be communicated to a skeptical world sensitively
yet without compromise. Courageously defending the gospel lovingly
and effectively while under attack or in the face of skepticism is a greater
ability than the ability to simply teach or preach a message to the friendly
stares of congregants.

Cutting it straight takes skill beyond preparing a Bible study or
sermon.

DIDAKTIKON

Did you know that Jesus is called "the Teacher" more than sixty times in
the Bible? We mustn't overlook the importance of knowing the Bible and
being able to communicate it decisively and effectively.

At first sight of the Greek word for teaching, *didaktikon*, I thought of
one of the characters from the *Transformers* movie franchise. *Didaktikon*
sounds like one of the evil Decepticons led by Megatron who battle the
earth-defending Autobots. Instead, Paul used this word for being "able to
teach" in 1 Timothy 3:2 and in Titus 1:9, where he wrote about "holding
fast the faithful word which is in accordance with the **teaching**, so that
he will be able both to exhort in sound doctrine and to refute those who
contradict."

Didaktikon also where we get the English word *didactic*, meaning
"intended to teach" or "to convey instruction and information in addi-
tion to serving another purpose (such as pleasure and entertainment)."[5]

As with a Decepticon, there's more to *didaktikon* than meets the eye.
It is much more than the ability to publicly teach or preach. Within it are
found several key ingredients. It describes the man who has a teachable

spirit and can teach others.[6] He is not only wise but willing and able to communicate his wisdom to others.[7]

Matthew Henry described this quality similarly, "One who is both able **and** willing to communicate to others the knowledge which God has given him; one who is fit to teach, **and** ready to take all opportunities of giving instruction; who is himself well instructed in the things of the kingdom of heaven, **and** is communicative of what he knows to others."[8]

Some facets of *didaktikon* rise to the top of what is required of the dialed in man.

He grows. The dialed in man has a teachable spirit that deeply desires to know the Bible more. He listens to and learns from others. He is passionate in his regular study of God's Word. He applies it to his life and writes it on his heart. Psalm 119:9–16 best describes his passion for the Word:

> How can a young man keep his way pure?
> By keeping it according to Your word.
> With all my heart I have sought You;
> Do not let me wander from Your commandments.
> Your word I have treasured in my heart,
> That I may not sin against You.
> Blessed are You, O LORD;
> Teach me Your statutes.
> With my lips I have told of
> All the ordinances of Your mouth.
> I have rejoiced in the way of Your testimonies,
> As much as in all riches.
> I will meditate on Your precepts

And regard Your ways.

I shall delight in Your statutes;

I shall not forget Your word.

He knows. Subsequently, he has a masterful understanding of the Bible. He knows it better than most. He knows it better than anyone else in his household. His excellent working knowledge of the Bible overflows into everything he does. He can't help it. It's the dominant force in his life.

He shows. The dialed in man has hidden God's Word in his heart, but not for long. He must share God's truths with others and does so whenever possible, whether that is in a formal church setting or with the grocery store clerk. The Word of God will not remain silent or hidden. He is compelled to share it.

He opposes. Last, he is willing to confront false teachings. Did you know that federal agents are trained to spot a counterfeit dollar by becoming experts at knowing what the real dollar looks and feels like? When knowing the Bible is our life, it is easy to spot and confront false teachings.[9]

Being *didaktikon*—able to teach—involves knowing the Bible, but I hope you see that it is much more than that.

Legend tells a sad story about the prince of Grenada, heir to the Spanish crown, who was sentenced to life in solitary confinement in Madrid's ancient filthy prison aptly called the "Place of the Skull." Men went in alive. Most came out in a box. The only thing given to the prince was a Bible, which became his only earthly possession.

After his death decades later, when guards cleaned out his cell they found some notes he had written using nails to mark the soft stone of the prison walls:

Psalm 118:8 is the middle verse of the Bible; Ezra 7:21
contains all the letters of the alphabet except the letter
j; the ninth verse of the eighth chapter of Esther is the
longest verse in the Bible; no word or name of more
than six syllables can be found in the Bible. [10]

I found it tragic that in over three decades of studying the Word of
God, the greatest literary word in history, he died having gleaned nothing
from it but useless trivia. Hebrews 4:12 reminds us of the supernatural
power in this culture-shifting work: "For the word of God is living and
active and sharper than any two-edged sword, and piercing as far as the
division of soul and spirit, of both joints and marrow, and able to judge
the thoughts and intentions of the heart."

But how many today, including those who attend church regularly,
think it is just a book and, like the prince of Grenada, never allow it to
penetrate their very souls?[11]

Having the ability to teach is more than raw knowledge or intellectual giftedness. A Jesus-formed heart creates passion *and* knowledge,
faith *and* action, emotions *and* understanding.

The dialed in man knows how to cut it straight.

DIAL IT IN
Small-Group Exercises

1. Read 2 Timothy 2:15. What is your greatest takeaway from this chapter?

2. What do Psalm 119:9–16, 105 teach? What other verses in Psalm 119 inspire you to master the Scriptures?

3. Why is the Bible compared to a sword in Ephesians 6:17, Hebrews 4:12, Revelation 1:16, and Revelation 2:12?

4. Why can the Bible be trusted (2 Tim. 3:16–17; 2 Pet. 1:20–21)?

5. How often do you study the Bible, what is your favorite method, and what are your recent discoveries?

6. What admonition and warning do you see in in 2 Timothy 4:1–4? How are you witnessing this today?

7. What do Matthew 28:20, Acts 2:42, and Romans 6:17 say about our role in teaching the Bible to others?

ASSESSING YOUR CAPACITY

For each of the ten assessment statements, rank yourself accordingly:

> (5) Strongly agree
>
> (4) Agree
>
> (3) Neither agree nor disagree
>
> (2) Disagree
>
> (1) Strongly disagree

Add up your total score at the bottom, then add the overall score in the appendix on page 290.

1. I regularly share my faith in Christ. _____

I often share what I have learned in the Bible. _____

My understanding of Jesus is clear, firm, and unshakable. _____

I do not get defensive when people challenge what I believe. _____

I never shy away from spiritual discussions for fear that I may not know enough. _____

I can find a Bible verse for virtually everything in life. _____

I would have no problem with teaching a Bible study. _____

The Bible is my great tool to help others find their best lives. _____

I have multiple life verses memorized. _____

I know the Bible better than anyone else in my family. _____

TOTAL SCORE _____

THE FAITHFUL MAN

Building Guardrails around Your Bride

A pair of [breasts] can pull a man further than a pair of oxen ever can.

—Bufe Karraker

Only the ugly are loyal.

—Lucius Annaeus Seneca, Roman Stoic philosopher and dramatist

WHEN IN ROME

Christianity stormed the world stage in one of the vilest, most sexualized times in world history. In many ways, the ancient world was in a state of moral chaos. The reason modern people view pornography, adultery, and sex outside of the marital covenant as sinful is because of Christianity. In the Greco-Roman world, even the highest positions and places in society were characterized by brutal immorality. It has been said that the only new virtue that Christianity brought into this world was chastity. The fledgling Christian church had to swim against the current to demon-strate chastity, stability, and the sanctity of the Christian home.

Christianity brought monogamy and faithfulness into the family and radically transformed how women were viewed by their born-again men. Christianity is the *single most freeing* religion to happen to women in the history of the world.

Speaking of women, Emperor Augustus once said, "If we could do without wives, we would be rid of a nuisance. But since nature has decreed that we can neither live comfortably with them nor live at all without them, we must look rather to our permanent interests than passing pleasure."[1]

"You can't live with them, and you can't live without them"—Augustus's words have become a familiar part of our culture's so-called wisdom.

According to Roman law, a wife had no rights—zero. A man could kill his wife if he caught her in adultery, but she could do nothing if she caught him doing the same! Polygamy and adultery were so common that Seneca stated bluntly, "Only the ugly are loyal."[2]

And it wasn't much better for Jewish women of the day. Josephus, a first-century Jewish historian, wrote, "By ancestral custom, a man can live with more than one wife.... With us [Jews] it is lawful for a husband to dissolve a marriage, but a wife, if she departs from her husband, cannot marry another, unless her former husband put her away."[3]

Christianity, then, was a radical paradigm shift back to the biblical view—God's view—of marriage: "For this reason a man shall leave his father and his mother, and be joined to his wife; and they shall become one flesh" (Gen. 2:24).

But the Greco-Roman laissez-faire view of women and marriage lingered in the church. Venus was the Roman goddess of love and beauty and the main deity of Corinth. Her temple was one of the most magnificent in the city, and it housed one thousand "priestesses" to Venus, who were publicly supported temple prostitutes who offered their services for the worship of Venus.

Talk about pastoral care!

It was common for married "Christian" men to have their cake and eat it too, which is what Paul vehemently rebuked Corinthian men for in 1 Corinthians 6:13–20. In the context of the ancient world and the Corinthian church, it all starts to make sense:

> Yet the body is not for immorality, but for the Lord, and the Lord is for the body. Now God has not only raised the Lord, but will also raise us up through His power. Do you not know that your bodies are members of Christ? Shall I then take away the members of Christ and make them members of a prostitute? May it never be! Or do you not know that the one who joins himself to a prostitute is one body with her? For He says, "The two shall become one flesh." But the one who joins himself to the Lord is one spirit with Him. Flee immorality. Every other sin that a man commits is outside the body, but the immoral man sins against his own body. Or do you not know that your body is a temple of the Holy Spirit who is in you, whom you have from God, and that you are not your own? For you

have been bought with a price: therefore glorify God in your body.

Sadly, we aren't too far from the moral state of the Corinthian church today, as false doctrines of grace, living together outside of marriage, and "discovering my truth" abound. I am reminded of Paul's words to the church in Rome, "What shall we say then? Are we to continue in sin so that grace may increase? May it never be! How shall we who died to sin still live in it?" (Rom. 6:1–2).

How shall the man who is saved build guardrails around his bride?

FAITHFUL DENIED

What do we mean by *faithful man*?

I had to laugh when a man I was talking to about the sanctity of marriage, to defend his point (I'm still not sure what his point was), made an oxymoronic declaration about faithfulness, "I'm a serial monogamist!" I didn't have the heart to correct him. When we discuss what faithful means here, most scholars agree that it means monogamy—only one wife—and the overseer must be completely faithful to his wife. He must be a loyal husband, preserving marriage with all its chastity according to Hebrews 13:4: "Marriage is to be held in honor among all, and the marriage bed is to be undefiled; for fornicators and adulterers God will judge."

Remember that the twenty qualities we are covering in this book were originally written as a standard by which to select spiritual leaders, which should be the goal of every Christian man. Although the qualifications and selection of spiritual leadership are vital to the church's witness, the process of selecting leaders in the church is not the focus of this book. Rather, this book aims to inspire all men to live at full capacity as the best version of themselves. In this chapter, we will not share opinions about who can be in leadership, nor will we share ministry practices regarding men who have committed adultery, been divorced or widowed, or never married.

The goal of this chapter is to help the man who is married, or one day will be, build guardrails around his bride.

LIGHTEST THING IN THE WORLD

Years ago, I heard a joke that I knew I'd never forget. Forgive the offense, but some things must be said.

> Question: Do you know why the male penis is the lightest thing in the world?
>
> Answer: Because it can be lifted with just a thought!

For those who are offended by that joke, consider what is worse: that joke or you with your pants down in front of a computer screen? Or even worse still, your pants on the floor of some dingy hotel with a woman who is not your wife? Your mind can take you down a road you don't want to travel, which is why we want to help you in the battle for the mind, taking every thought captive (2 Cor. 10:5).

Alluding to Jesus' words, C. S. Lewis once joked, "He that but looketh on a plate of ham and eggs to lust after it, hath already committed breakfast with it in his heart."[4] But what did Jesus mean?

> You have heard that it was said, "You shall not commit adultery"; but I say to you that everyone who looks at a

woman with lust for her has already committed adultery
with her in his heart. If your right eye makes you stumble,
tear it out and throw it from you; for it is better for you
to lose one of the parts of your body, than for your whole
body to be thrown into hell. If your right hand makes
you stumble, cut it off and throw it from you; for it is
better for you to lose one of the parts of your body, than
for your whole body to go into hell. (Matt. 5:27–30)

The Greek word for "lust" in this passage is *epithymia*. Lust is a strong
craving or desire for someone or something. Though it's infrequently
used—only twenty-nine times in Scripture—a common theme is seen
in each case. The word *lust* is never used in a positive context. It's always
seen in a negative light, especially when it refers to a strong desire that is
negative and forbidden.

My friend and ministry partner from many years ago, the late Rich
Fisher, loved basketball and had the heart to mentor young single guys
like I once was. As single Jim Ramos listening to a married guy, I took
his advice: "You played basketball. Remember the three seconds in the
key violation? Three in the key. Never look at a woman more than three
seconds or it's a violation." In other words, when your look turns into a
leer, you've crossed the line. When the adoration of God's masterpiece
turns into objectification, sin has entered the building.

I still take his wisdom to heart.

During that time, I began a regiment of praying for and over my
future wife, saving myself until the night we married. Since my sons were
toddlers, I have been praying daily for their wives and the fruit of those
prayers is coming to fruition as I type these words.

Lust is not only to desire a woman in an illicit sexual relationship but also to think in terms of how to cause it to happen. Lust has a plan of action attached to it, which differentiates lust as a temptation from lust as a sin.[5] *Merriam-Webster* defines lust as "usually intense or unbridled sexual desire" and "an intense longing."[6]

The best way I've found to prevent lust is to establish guardrails against it. In Deuteronomy 22:8, God says, "When you build a new house, you shall make a parapet for your roof, so that you will not bring bloodguilt on your house if anyone falls from it."

Did you catch that? Guardrails were built to protect those you love. Guardrails may upset some people. Who cares? Your job is to protect those you love—from you! Start building your guardrails now.

BUILD GUARDRAILS

Out of all the fifty team meetings in my five-volume *Strong Men Series Study Guide*, the meeting on guardrails is a perennial favorite. In it, I list ten marriage-saving guardrails that will keep you between the lines. Like highway guardrails, they aren't meant to be pretty or scenic but to direct and protect you—from **yourself**!

Here are some ways to preserve the life of your marriage.

Guardrail 1: Never develop an emotional connection to a person of the opposite sex. If your job requires you to work near women, keep all conversations professional and work related. Purge your social media platforms of ex-girlfriends and women who you could become attracted to in an unhealthy way, and do not start conversations with any of them!

Guardrail 2: Never be alone with a person of the opposite sex unless at work with an open door and window. My friend Tim is the senior vice president of a large insurance company, and he practices this guardrail religiously. Do not tell me it is impossible for you. That is a cop-out.

Guardrail 3: Never engage in any negative talk about your spouse with a person of the opposite sex. I have witnessed dozens of men fall into adultery, and it all started with negative talk about their wives and a woman saying, "If I had a man like you, I would never treat you that way."

Guardrail 4: Never compliment a person of the opposite sex in a way that would elicit an emotional response.

Guardrail 5: Never have counseling or mentoring relationships with a person of the opposite sex. I know of a pastor who was militant about never meeting with people for more than thirty minutes until the worship pastor's beautiful wife asked him to mentor her. Their meetings increased to nearly two hours at times. Thankfully he was confronted by his insightful youth pastor before the emotional affair got physical.

Guardrail 6: Never make physical contact beyond a casual handshake or quick side hug with a person of the opposite sex.

Guardrail 7: Never make foul, rude, coarse, or sexual comments, *especially* to a person of the opposite sex. Sexual or rude talk is a gateway to adultery.

Guardrail 8: Never give a gift or card to a person of the opposite sex that is only from you. Say "we" a lot, referring to you and your wife. There is no need for you to ever personally recognize or affirm a woman in writing unless it is your wife.

Guardrail 9: Never engage in conversation about personal details with a person of the opposite sex without your wife being present.

Guardrail 10: Never assume your spouse is living by your standards! I know a Christian man who thought his Christian wife was following the same standards that he was only to be broken by her barhopping with the girls. Shanna can check my phone and computer history whenever she wants. I can do the same with hers. Knowing this is freeing.[7]

SMARTPHONES AND DUMB GUYS

Before marrying Shanna, I came across an alarming picture of her. It was a picture taken in the late afternoon in Santa Barbara, California, next to a green street sign that said "Haley Street" (Haley is her maiden name). I was alarmed by how skinny she was and the sadness in her beautiful green eyes.

"That picture was taken right after I found out my boyfriend was cheating on me with my best friend and college roommate. They ended up getting married."

It was then that I vowed never to hurt her like that. And I haven't. I've been faithful to Shanna from three years before I met her (1989) until now, and with God's help, I will remain faithful until I graduate to heaven.

But that doesn't mean lust is not a struggle. It has been. It still is. I like to joke that 99 percent of men battle lust and the other 1 percent lie about it. If you are a man with a smartphone, I beg you to join all Men in the Arena staff members and directors and protect the smart devices you own with accountability software or any effective browser filter. It is a game changer.

Let's end with another joke.

Question: What do you call a guy with an unprotected smartphone?

Answer: A dumb guy.

Build guardrails around your bride.

DIAL IT IN
Small-Group Exercises

1. Discuss Genesis 2:24, Matthew 19:4–6, and 1 Timothy 3:2 in the context of faithfulness.

2. Review how moral purity was a new Christian virtue in ancient Greco-Roman culture. How do you think 1 Corinthians 6:13–20 would have been received by men at the time? Women?

3. Discuss your sex life (if you feel comfortable doing so) in light of Proverbs 5:18–20, 1 Corinthians 7:1–5, and Hebrews 13:4. Rank your sex life (considering frequency and quality) from 1 to 10, and tell why you ranked it so.

4. When does a look turn to lust? What do Proverbs 16:17, Matthew 5:27–30, and 2 Corinthians 10:5 teach us about finding victory over lust?

5. Reflect on Deuteronomy 22:8. Which one of the guardrails listed in this chapter have you broken recently? Who knows about it?

6. Read 1 Corinthians 10:13. What strategies have you implemented to guard yourself against lust?

ASSESSING YOUR CAPACITY

For each of the ten assessment statements, rank yourself accordingly:

(5) Strongly agree

(4) Agree

(3) Neither agree nor disagree

(2) Disagree

(1) Strongly disagree

Add up your total score at the bottom, then add the overall score in the appendix on page 269.

1. I follow strict moral boundaries to ensure my
fidelity.   _____

My wife would say that I consider her the most
important person to me.   _____

I never look at pornography.   _____

I have built accountability safeguards into my electronic devices.   _____

I believe divorce is not an option.   _____

I have never had an emotional connection with a
woman other than my wife.   _____

I do not masturbate to illicit images or memories.   _____

My wife and I make love regularly.   _____

I do not leer at other women.   _____

I never have and never will cheat on my wife.   _____

TOTAL SCORE   _____

THE JUST MAN

Do What Is Right Even When It Isn't Popular

Justice is truth in action.

—Benjamin Disraeli

He has told you, O man, what is good;
And what does the LORD require of you
But to do justice, to love kindness,
And to walk humbly with your God?

—Micah 6:8

LIFE'S NOT FAIR

We joke with our adult sons that their names should have been What, Huh, and Why. Colton was born with hearing issues that we discovered after his first four years of asking us to repeat everything we said.

"What?"

Darby, being the middle son and only introvert in the family, thought that if he could disappear from our parenting field of vision, he could do whatever he wanted. When confronted with negative behaviors, he would play dumb, try to disappear, and hope we would direct the discipline he deserved to one of his brothers. Instead of answering us, he'd postpone the inevitable.

"Huh?"

James, our oldest, is a great salesman. A month after graduating from college he became a campaign manager for the Republican Party in Oregon, which usually means a landslide loss. But his candidate won for state representative by a large margin. He could sell oceanfront property in Wyoming. As a child, he wanted to know the reasons for every decision.

"Why? Why do I have to do that?"

The phrase they despised growing up is coming back to haunt them as they start families of their own, plagiarized from our playbook: "Because I said so." (If I had a dollar for every time I said that!)

"Because I said so" was my favorite saying in this world where parents don't make their children work to earn things they do not need. My sons were given high-mileage first vehicles by their grandparents, while many of their peers were given newer cars than Shanna and I owned and told this great lie: "School is your work. As long as you're in school, you won't need to get a job."

Huh?

Conversely, my sons were mandated to work to pay for their insurance and gas, play multiple varsity sports, attend church activities, and maintain high grade point averages, while many of their peers were given a free ride to Entitlement Town. My sons argued that they wished we had more money because "This isn't fair!"

"What did you say?" I would ask, positioning myself awkwardly close to the complaining son's face. "Life isn't fair. Even if we were multimillionaires, you'd still drive these old cars and work to pay for it all. Do you know why? Because I am the meanest dad in the world. I love you. Now, get to work! You will thank me later."

Life isn't fair. People win, and people lose. People live long and happy lives, and people live horribly and die too soon. Children are born in affluent nations, and children are born in underdeveloped countries. Some children are nurtured by loving families, and babies are butchered through abortion. I can go on and on.

Life isn't just or fair.

But the dialed in man is fair, just, and righteous. He does the right thing even when it's not popular. Someone said, "Only dead things drift downstream." But the dialed-in man is willing to put in the sweat equity. He doesn't whine about what should be coming to him. He doesn't demand reparations. He does what is right even if that means swimming upstream, cutting against the grain, or standing among the minority. I love what Chuck Swindoll wrote, "I've lived my life under the conviction that the majority is usually wrong, and that belief has served me well."[1]

The dialed in man acknowledges and embraces this fact with great pleasure.

I once read a saying that was transformational for me: "Evil prevails when good men do nothing." It takes a dialed in man to stand up for justice, treat all people fairly, show no favoritism, and speak on behalf of God and the powerless and against the evils of society.

Do what is right, even if it isn't popular.

RIGHTWISE

In Titus 1:7–8 we come to our next quality of the dialed in man, "For the overseer must be … **just**." In Titus 1:8 the word Paul used for "just" was *dikaios*. Amazingly, *dikaios* appears over two hundred times in the New Testament, and the Hebrew for "just"—*tzedek*—appears over five hundred times in the Old Testament!

Wow! Do you think justice matters to God?

Interestingly, in 1526 when William Tyndale translated the Bible into English, he translated *dikaios* in Titus 1:8 to "rightwise" or "rightways," which we know as "righteousness."

Dikaios means "without prejudice or partiality."[2] According to Thayer's Greek Lexicon, the word also has both *horizontal* and *vertical* connotations: "Observing divine and human laws."[3] This will be important later. I love the cross illustration to explain this twofold understanding of righteousness.

Horizontally, the Greeks use *dikaios* to describe a person "who gives both to other people and to the gods what is due them …. who give to other people the respect, and to God the reverence which are their due."[4] *Dikaios* describes the man who is just and upright in his dealings with all.[5]

Vertically, this quality includes giving God His due as Lord of all. The man with this characteristic has found salvation through Jesus Christ and has given God his full capacity—he trusts God completely. Not only does he surrender everything to the Savior, but he also makes a public stand to bear witness to what he believes and why. To stay silent about our faith is not only cowardly but denies God what is due Him, as Paul said, "For I am not ashamed of the gospel, for it is the power of God for salvation to everyone who believes" (Rom. 1:16).

We will unpack this more later. Do what is right, even if it isn't popular.

Here is a gruesome example of a just man who did something that was not popular.

HORIZONTALLY JUST

In the seventh century BC, Zaleucus, the legendary king of Greece, decreed that all adulterers should be punished with the loss of both their eyes. Not long after this decree, his son was caught in adultery, but to show parental responsibility, he maintained the decree that two eyes be removed. In an incredible act of justice, King Zaleucus shared the penalty with his son by ordering one of his own eyes to be thrust out along with one of his sons![6]

James the Just (also known as James the brother of the Lord and James the Righteous) was the half brother of Jesus and an early leader in the Jerusalem church who died a martyr around AD 65. The author of the book of James, he spent more time on the sin of partiality in James 2:1–10 than any other New Testament writer:

> My brethren, do not hold your faith in our glorious
> Lord Jesus Christ with an attitude of personal favorit-
> ism. For if a man comes into your assembly with a gold
> ring and dressed in fine clothes, and there also comes
> in a poor man in dirty clothes, and you pay special
> attention to the one who is wearing the fine clothes,
> and say, "You sit here in a good place," and you say to
> the poor man, "You stand over there, or sit down by
> my footstool," have you not made distinctions among

yourselves, and become judges with evil motives? Listen, my beloved brethren: did not God choose the poor of this world to be rich in faith and heirs of the kingdom which He promised to those who love Him? But you have dishonored the poor man. Is it not the rich who oppress you and personally drag you into court? Do they not blaspheme the fair name by which you have been called?

If, however, you are fulfilling the royal law according to the Scripture, "You shall love your neighbor as yourself," you are doing well. But if you show partiality, you are committing sin and are convicted by the law as transgressors. For whoever keeps the whole law and yet stumbles in one point, he has become guilty of all.

Are you showing favoritism to a person or people group? What advantage does a person gain by receiving something they did not earn? What happens when they have to work at something, such as maintaining a healthy marriage, raising a family, or moving upward through their career?

Martin Luther King Jr. had something to say about favoritism: "I have a dream that my four little children will one day live in a nation where they will not be judged by the color of their skin but by the content of their character."[7] Favoritism judges based on outward position, status, or appearance, but we should judge others based on the fruit they produce: "But the LORD said to Samuel, 'Do not look at his appearance or at the height of his stature, because I have rejected him; for God sees not as man sees, for man looks at the outward appearance, but the LORD looks at the heart'" (1 Sam. 16:7).

The fair, just, and righteous man deals with people the way he would like them to treat him—the Golden Rule (Matt. 7:12). Do not bring your prejudices, biases, or predispositions to any person or situation. Instead, let the actions and character of others speak for themselves. Do what is right, even if it isn't popular.

VERTICAL JUSTICE, GOD'S JUSTICE

You've seen that there are two sides of the just man—horizontal and vertical. Earlier, we discussed being able to teach, but there is a distinction between the man who can and the man who does, the one who thinks and the one who acts, the man who sits and the man who stands. The just man is willing to take a stand for his vertical beliefs.

Billy Graham is believed to have said, "Courage is contagious. When a brave man takes a stand, the spines of others are often stiffened." More than sin, hardship, or spiritual pedigree, courage is the *distinction* that separates the strong from the weak, missionaries from mission fields, and men who thrive spiritually from those who backslide.

We see this manifested in the book of Acts: "But Peter, taking his stand with the eleven, raised his voice and declared to them: 'Men of Judea and all you who live in Jerusalem, let this be known to you and give heed to my words'" (2:14).

One group that took a stand was the Knights Templar, which thrived from 1129 to 1312. In their distinctive white mantles with red crosses, they were among the most skilled fighting units in the Crusades. What people don't know is that 90 percent of Templars were noncombatant members who managed a large economic infrastructure throughout Christendom.[8] But they are most notably remembered for the Crusades.

Legend and controversy have surrounded the order of the Knights Templar, but they will be remembered, good or bad, as defenders of the faith. Where are the knights of today? Where are the men who will stand against the diabolical lies of the Enemy and give God His due? Daniel Webster penned, "Justice ... is the great interest of man on Earth. It is the ligament which holds civilized beings and civilized nations together."[9]

I wholeheartedly agree. I believe in biblical justice—the justice of God. Where is the just man? Where is the champion for the weak and powerless? Who will stand for them? Who will be the voice for those who have none? When the just man stands up to defend God's Word, he may be canceled, he may be ridiculed, and he may be persecuted. But the just man stands, nonetheless. A passage every man should commit to *memory* is 1 Peter 3:14–16:

> But even if you should suffer for the sake of **righteousness**, you are blessed. And do not fear their intimidation, and do not be troubled, but sanctify Christ as Lord in your hearts, always being ready to make a defense to everyone who asks you to give an account for the hope that is in you, yet with gentleness and reverence; and keep a good conscience so that in the thing in which you are slandered, those who revile your good behavior in Christ will be put to shame.

Dialed in men valiantly represent God (vertical) and other people (horizontal). Refusing to shrink back, they openly defend the truths of God (Heb. 10:39). Do what is right, even if it isn't popular, just as the three boys in Daniel 3:16–18 did what was right even though they were facing the furnace for what they believed.

> Shadrach, Meshach, and Abed-nego replied to the king, "O Nebuchadnezzar, we do not need to give you an answer concerning this matter. If it be so, our God whom we serve is able to deliver us from the furnace of blazing fire; and He will deliver us out of your hand, O king. But **even if He does not**, let it be known to you, O king, that we are not going to serve your gods or worship the golden image that you have set up."

JUST MAN OR JUST A MAN?

Shadrach, Meshach, and Abed-nego were willing to put their faith in the fire. They were willing to burn for their cause. Are you? Are you a just man? Or are you just a man? Here is a way to find out. In the chapter on "The Generous Man," we learned that we are simply managers of God's resources. Those resources include our time, talents, and treasures. How much of your God-entrusted resources go to kingdom causes that you care deeply about?

The just man is a wrecked man. He is passionate about specific injustices in the world, and he gives his time, talents, and treasures to eradicate them. It is one thing to get angry when we read about little children being trafficked as sex slaves. It is quite the other to act. Shanna and I are passionate about a baby's right to life, so we give to support the fight against abortion.

What wrecks you? What provokes you to take an active role in curing an injustice in the world—racism, abortion, sex trafficking, lost souls, pornography, drug or alcohol addiction, or domestic abuse? The list goes on. There are a myriad of noble kingdom causes out there. Which ones is God calling you to invest your resources to eradicate? Start there.

Do what is right, even if it costs you greatly. Do what is right even if it hurts. Get dialed in.

DIAL IT IN
Small-Group Exercises

1. In your own words, explain the Greek word *dikaios* and its relationship to being just, fair, and righteous.

2. What are some insights about vertical justice you see in Matthew 28:18–20, Romans 1:16, and Hebrews 10:39?

3. What does James 2:1–10 teach us about how to deal with people of different ages, religions, races, or political views?

4. Why is this difficult? Which group do you struggle with being biased against the most, and how will you repent of this prejudice?

5. What do 1 Samuel 16:7 and Matthew 7:12, 16–20 teach us about how to treat people fairly?

6. What is the difference between those who can teach the Bible and those who stand up for what it says (2 Tim. 4:1–3; 1 Pet. 3:14–16)?

7. Discuss your insights from Daniel 3:16–18 and 2 Timothy 3:12 and how you will implement them in your life.

ASSESSING YOUR CAPACITY

For each of the ten assessment statements, rank yourself accordingly:

> (5) Strongly agree
>
> (4) Agree
>
> (3) Neither agree nor disagree
>
> (2) Disagree
>
> (1) Strongly disagree

Add up your total score at the bottom, then add the overall score in the appendix on page 291.

1. I judge a person by their character more than their color, religion, or appearance. _____

I am known as someone who is fair. _____

I never show favoritism toward others. _____

I discern right from wrong and lead those I love toward good. _____

I care more about doing what is right than getting my way. _____

People seek me out for wise counsel in difficult situations. _____

I do not offer advice until I hear both sides of the story. _____

I get angry when I see people being treated unfairly. _____

I believe that the strong should protect the weak at all costs, and I practice this belief. _____

I challenge those who misrepresent the truth. _____

TOTAL SCORE _____

THE GENTLE MAN

Be a Gentle Giant among Men

All who are truly godly and are real disciples of Christ have a gentle spirit in them.

—Jonathan Edwards

It's the strong hand, not the weak one, that must learn to be gentle.

—Gary Thomas

A GIANT AMONG MEN

I've interviewed hundreds of great men. Men who have founded denominations, built global ministries, and sold millions of books. But one stands above the rest. Wess Stafford was the president of Compassion International. Under his leadership, Compassion grew to a 500-million-dollar annual budget (84 percent of which went directly to children), with 2.5 million children sponsored globally. Wess is a real man's man, a US Army veteran, and an avid outdoorsman.

He has been awarded five honorary doctorates and has dined with presidents of multiple countries. His passion for children originates from his missionary days in Africa when he witnessed many of his childhood friends dying of easily treatable diseases. In an emotional moment on the *Men in the Arena* podcast, Stafford admitted, "I'm always seconds away from crying over children."[1]

Stafford would gladly trade all he has achieved to share breadcrumbs with a child. He can stand with any man but prefers to stoop to pick up a child. His ability to pour gentleness from a position of strength is why he embodies the spirit of gentleness that theologian Jonathan Edwards described when he wrote, "All who are truly godly and are real disciples of Christ have a gentle spirit in them."[2]

The next quality of the dialed in man can be summarized in one word: **gentle**. Let's dive in to discover what Paul meant by this obscure word.

GENTLE AS *EPIEIKES*

Paul used the Greek word *epieikes* to describe this masculine quality that is only mentioned five times in the New Testament. The New American Standard Bible uses the word *gentle* twenty times, but *epieikes* is used on only five of those occasions (Phil. 4:5; 1 Tim. 3:3; Titus 3:2; James 3:17; 1 Pet. 2:18). The problem is that *epieikes* is "another of these completely untranslatable words."[3] Anglican archbishop Richard Trench (1807–1886) described *epieikeia* as "'retreating from the letter of right better to preserve the spirit of right' and is 'the spirit which recognizes the impossibility of cleaving to all formal law ... that recognizes the danger that ever waits upon the assertion of legal rights, lest they should be pushed into moral wrongs ... the spirit which rectifies and redresses the **injustice of justice**.'"[4]

2226226226226226

I'm tempted to defer to other English translations of "gentle" from two similar Greek words and try to weave them into this chapter. The Greek *prautes* was used in Jesus' famous Sermon on the Mount: "Blessed are the gentle"—translated as "meek" in the NIV—"for they shall inherit the earth" (Matt. 5:5). Another use of *prautes* that has deeply impacted my life is Matthew 11:28–30:

> Come to Me, all who are weary and heavy-laden, and I will give you rest. Take My yoke upon you and learn from Me, for I am **gentle** and humble in heart, and you will find rest for your souls. For My yoke is easy and My burden is light.

Epios is yet another word often translated as "gentle." In 1 Thessalonians 2:7, we read, "But we proved to be **gentle** among you, as a nursing mother tenderly cares for her own children." Then again, in 2 Timothy 2:24–25, "The Lord's bond-servant must not be quarrelsome, but be kind to all, able to teach, patient when wronged, with gentleness correcting those who are in opposition, if perhaps God may grant them repentance leading to the knowledge of the truth."

The dialed in man is a gentle giant.

GENTLE GIANTS

Gentle. Meek. Mild. Humble.

Words are often interchanged in Scripture to describe gentleness. Sadly, they are often interpreted by readers to mean being weak, soft, timid, and cowardly. Nothing could be further from the truth. Jerry Bridges wrote, "Both gentleness and meekness are born of power, not weakness."[5]

Did you catch that?

The act of gentleness can *only* manifest from a position of strength. Being gentle means humbling yourself and making yourself strategically smaller to care for those who are weaker, smaller, or younger. It can look like setting aside your power or position, as Jesus did for us in coming to earth in the form of a man (Phil. 2:3–10), or kneeling to honor a child, as Wess Stafford did.

Only a man of strength can be a gentle giant since gentleness flows from a position of strength. Only a large man can stoop to bless someone less in stature or fortune. Maybe that is why so many males today do not know how to show gentleness to their wives, children, or those who are less fortunate. They aren't men at all, but mere males masquerading as men. You can read more about that in my book *Strong Men Dangerous Times*.

You cannot give what you do not possess. A man can only give what his capacity allows and can handle. Gentleness cannot manifest from a position of weakness. It is a manifestation of strength. What can the man holding a cardboard sign, begging for money, offer to the adjacent man of means who waits awkwardly for the light to turn green? How can the rambunctious toddler care for his mother? *Gentle* (*epieikes*) describes something offered from a position of strength. The gentlest men on the planet are the strongest—whole, not broken, operating at high capacity. The gentle man is a gentle giant of a man. He is dialed in.

BROKEN HALOS

I love the story about the man who went to the doctor's office with a severe headache that wouldn't go away.

"Doc, I have this intense pain that goes all around my head. I can't sleep. I've tried every legal drug I can think of, and nothing works. Can you help me? Please! I'm begging you."

"No problem," the doctor said, "but first I want to ask you a few questions to dial in my diagnosis. Do you drink a lot of alcohol ever?"

"Booze?" said the man angrily. "I'm a Christian. I would never touch that sinful stuff!"

"How about smoking?"

"Cancer sticks? Have you seen the kind of people that smoke? I would never even associate with smokers, let alone touch that stuff! What kind of person willingly subjects themselves to an ashtray mouth?"

"I hate to ask this, so please don't be offended, but you know how some guys are. Have you ever been with another woman, who isn't your wife, in a sexual way?"

"Of course not! What kind of loser do you think I am? I get up every morning, read my Bible, pray, go to work, and get to bed by nine o'clock every night."

"Okay, that helps a lot. Tell me. Is the pain sharp and localized, an endless throbbing, or more of a pain that shoots from the outside of your head inward?"

"Yes, that's it, Doc! Thank you. It is the sharp, shooting kind that never goes away."

"Simple, my good man. The problem is that your halo is on too tight. All we need to do is loosen it up a bit."

My halo gets a little tight at times. How about yours?

If only halos came as snapbacks, right?

How often do you have thoughts that are nothing more than one snap tighter on the halo and one step further from Jesus, one step further away from being a gentle representative of Jesus and displaying your full capacity to a world that desperately needs it?

Look at the father embracing his humiliated son. Listen to Jesus calling an undignified tax collector in a tree to come down. Feel the emotion in the leper touched by Jesus, the demon-possessed man Jesus set free, or the woman humiliated by sin whom Jesus chose not to condemn. Over and over, we see Jesus fixing broken halos.

He loves welding broken halos.

He mends broken halos and breaks prideful halos.

There are only three times that Jesus was visibly angry; one of them is in Mark 10:13–16.

> And they were bringing children to Him so that He might touch them; but the disciples rebuked them. But when Jesus saw this, **He was indignant** and said to them, "Permit the children to come to Me; do not hinder them; for the kingdom of God belongs to such as these. Truly I say to you, whoever does not receive the kingdom of God like a child will not enter it at all." And He took them in His arms and began blessing them, laying His hands on them.

Can you sense the anger, gentleness, and excitement in the crowd that day? Gentle Jesus can both be angry and gentle at the same time. He may be gentle Jesus, but make no mistake about it, He is not Jell-O Jesus. Brennan Manning wrote, "In New Testament times the child was considered of no importance, meriting little attention or favor. 'Children in that society had no status at all—they did not count.' The child was regarded with scorn."[6]

But Jesus counts those who do not count. That is what a gentle man does. He leverages his strength on behalf of another's weakness. The dialed in man blesses the world with the full weight of who he is.

Can you sense the full emotion of Jesus' gentleness (yes, gentleness) one Sabbath in the temple? "After looking around at them **with anger**, grieved at their hardness of heart, He said to the man, 'Stretch out your hand.' And he stretched it out, and his hand was restored" (Mark 3:5).

Jesus made those with broken halos feel at home in His presence. About Jesus' gentleness, Jerry Bridges wrote, "Christ's whole demeanor was such that people were often restful in his presence. This effect is another outworking of the grace of gentleness. People are at rest, or ease, around the Christian who is truly gentle."[7]

How do those with broken halos feel around you? Wait, that's the wrong question. The right one is, How do you feel around those with broken halos?

Become the gentle giant of a man God intends for you to be.

RAGAMUFFIN GENTILE

Study Jesus' responses to people in the Gospels, and you may be surprised. He offered a gentle spirit of grace to the seemingly unspiritual—those with broken halos. But He blasted Mosaic law when talking to religious leaders with tight halos.

Why? Because those who seemed unspiritual knew their halos were broken, unlike the proud who had their stuff together: "Why do you look at the speck that is in your brother's eye, but do not notice the log that is in your own eye? Or how can you say to your brother, 'Let me take the speck out of your eye,' and behold, the log is in your own eye?" (Matt. 7:3–4).

When we talk about displaying our gentle strength to those who have less than us, who are we talking about? Think hard about different groups and how you outwardly respond (or refuse to respond) to each. If you're unclear, talk to your wife, children, or someone else who sees your life in real time.

Politically opposed. I follow Jesus before all things. I'm a Jesus-follower before I am an American, Canadian, African, Australian, or Italian. Do you get the point? Our identity is in Jesus, period. Not Jesus, plus. Our life is wrapped up in Him! To withhold a spirit of gentleness from those with diametrically opposing political views is nothing less than diabolical. Check yourself and your political opinions at the door. At some point, followers of Jesus must educate themselves and realize that most of what they see on national news, besides the weather, is a show, fake, fiction. It is like World Wrestling Entertainment (WWE). It is fun to watch, but it is not real.

Physically weaker. The only disciple that we know was married was Peter, who wrote, "You husbands in the same way, live with your wives in an understanding way, as with someone weaker, since she is a woman; and show her honor" (1 Pet. 3:7). Generally speaking, women are smaller, have a higher fat percentage and less muscle mass, are physically less explosive, and are emotionally cyclical. They possess many amazing qualities that men generally do not and in many ways are superior to us guys. But knowing this truth is a mandate to show greater honor and gentleness, not hubris and judgment.

The same goes for anyone who is physically weaker—those with disabilities, those who are underdeveloped physically, and those who are elderly. Paul Eldridge once said, "A man is most accurately judged by how he treats those who are not in a position either to retaliate or to reciprocate."[8]

Terminally and chronically ill. Some people suffer from chronic or terminal illnesses. Jesus never shrunk back from people who suffered. He embraced them. The gentle man does as well.

Spiritually enslaved. I've served God in full-time ministry since 1990, and quite honestly, at times, people annoy me. At times, I annoy myself! I can be overly critical of the life choices of others. When I am like this, my spirit leads me to dark places. We all should take to heart what a good friend reminded me: "People are not the enemy. They are held captive by him." They need a gentle hand of redirection.

Demographically downtrodden. You know who I'm talking about. I must check myself. I don't know their story, where they came from, or why they are where they are now.

Vocationally subordinate. How do you treat those who work for you? If you are in management, pastor a church, or lead a group of volunteers, how you handle personal stress, frustration, and failure is noticed. Would those you supervise be shocked to know that you follow Jesus? Do you humbly admit and fix your mistakes? Are you a good witness for Jesus at work?

DIAL IT IN
Small-Group Exercises

1. Read Matthew 7:1–5. Of the groups mentioned at the conclusion of this chapter, which one do you struggle to be gentle with, and why?

2. Read Philippians 3:20. Where have you faded from being a citizen of heaven first, and how has that hindered your ability to show gentleness?

3. Look at the three times Jesus got angry (Mark 3:1–5; 10:13–16; John 2:13–25). What kinds of things make Jesus angry?

4. Where did He demonstrate gentleness in each of these stories?

5. What picture of God's gentleness can you see in these broken-halo stories: Matthew 8:1–3, Mark 5:1–13, Luke 15:11–31, Luke 19:1–10, and John 8:1–11?

6. Look up the five times *epieikes* is translated as "gentle" in the Bible, in Philippians 4:5, 1 Timothy 3:2–3, Titus 3:2, James 3:17, and 1 Peter 2:18. What do you learn about gentleness from these passages?

ASSESSING YOUR CAPACITY

For each of the ten assessment statements, rank yourself accordingly:

> (5) Strongly agree
>
> (4) Agree
>
> (3) Neither agree nor disagree
>
> (2) Disagree
>
> (1) Strongly disagree

Add up your total score at the bottom, then add the overall score in the appendix on page 292.

1. I am careful not to inflict guilt or shame upon someone when they make a mistake. _____

I am sensitive to the feelings of others. _____

I have never been told I am too abrasive. _____

I am the first to offer a prayer or listening ear when someone is hurting. _____

I weep with those who hurt. _____

I ask people I have hurt for forgiveness. _____

I do not lose my cool with those closest to me. _____

I have been called a gentle man. _____

I encourage people rather than criticize them. _____

Hurting people come to me for comfort. _____

TOTAL SCORE _____

THE DISCIPLINED MAN

Make Decisions against Yourself

He who sweats more in training bleeds less in war.

—Spartan saying

[Christ] wants a child's heart, but a grown-up's head.

—C. S. Lewis

DIALED IN BOOKENDS

I strategically made this chapter and "The Blameless Man" chapter the literal bookends of *Dialed In*. Remember back in chapter 1, I told you that being blameless, or above reproach, was the umbrella over the other nineteen qualities of the man who is living at full capacity. But without discipline, it all falls apart. A man will never live a blameless life without discipline over his thoughts, feelings, and actions. The first and last chapters of this book are like vise clamps holding the other eighteen together.

The disciplined man does not allow the immediate to undermine the ultimate. Often initiating his suffering to achieve his ultimate end, he makes decisions against his present desires for future results.

Blamelessness and discipline are mutually inclusive; without one, the other falls apart.

It's like the story of a guy who died and met Saint Peter at the pearly gates. Saint Peter asked him, "Have you ever done anything brave or noteworthy in your life?"

"Well, yes, one thing comes to mind," the man responded. "Once I walked up on a gang of rough-looking bikers as they were harassing a pretty young woman. I demanded that they take their hands off her, but they wouldn't listen. So, I approached the biggest, meanest-looking tattooed guy, who was their leader, and punched him in the throat. After that, I tipped his bike over, ripped off his nose ring, and threw it back in his face. Then I pointed my finger at all of them and said, 'Leave her alone or you'll have to answer to me!'"

Impressed, Saint Peter responded, "Wow! That is amazing! When did all of this happen?"

"Oh, about five minutes ago," the man replied.

He tried to be blameless, but the poor guy couldn't control his words and emotions. At least he went to heaven. Maybe he should have used a little more discipline over his words! In chapter 1, we discussed that the overarching theme of the full-capacity man is blamelessness, and now we strategically end with this chapter on discipline. With wisdom, a man will live at his full capacity by considering the circumstances surrounding his actions, making decisions against himself, and living a blameless life.

In 1 Timothy 3:2, Paul used a unique word that can be translated in many ways, one of which is "prudent."

Wikipedia explains prudence as "the ability to govern and discipline oneself by use of reason. It is classically considered to be ... one of the four cardinal virtues."[1] It is showing care and thought for the future. *Merriam-Webster* describes the prudent as, "Marked by wisdom or judiciousness. Shrewd in the management of practical affairs. Marked by circumspection: discreet."[2]

If Stephen Covey were alive today, he would probably say that the prudent man will "begin with the end in mind."[3] He "play[s] the movie," as Henry Cloud might affirm.[4] The prudent man is willing to make decisions against himself and his immediate desires to achieve a better future. He is willing to forgo the immediate for the ultimate. Financial expert Dave Ramsey likes to say, "If you will live like no one else, later you can live **like** no one else."[5]

But there is more to wisdom than initially meets the eye. Let's explore the word in the original Greek.

SOPHRON

The Greek word *sophron* is frustrating because it's hard to nail down. It reminds me of a story about a young businessman who was appointed to be president of a bank. The promotion was thrilling and intimidating—he was just thirty-two. So he made an appointment with the bank's board chairman to get advice about becoming an exemplary bank president.

"What is the most important thing for me to do as the new president?" he asked the older, wiser man.

"Make the right decisions," the older man nonchalantly responded.

"Thank you, sir. That is very helpful," the young man said, "but can you give me some more details? For example, how do I learn how to make right decisions?"

The chairman answered, "Experience."

Losing patience by now, the young man said, "But sir, how do I get experience?"

"Wrong decisions," the chairman explained.[6]

Like the young president who struggled to pin down the right way to lead, we can have a difficult time defining *sophron* because the word is translated many different ways.

For example, depending on the passage, the New International Version translates *sophron* as "temperate" (1 Tim. 3:11; Titus 2:2), "self-controlled" (1 Tim. 3:2), "sober" (1 Thess. 5:6, 8), and "right mind" (2 Cor. 5:13). Other Bible translations use the words "prudent" (NASB), "sober" (KJV), "discreet" (Darby), "sensible" (HCSB), and "sober-minded" (NKJV).

Kenneth Wuest defined it as "soberminded, serious, earnest."[7] William Barclay sounds exasperated by *sophron* in his explanation.

> We have translated *sōphrōn* as *prudent*, but it is virtu-
> ally **untranslatable**. It is variously translated as *of
> sound mind, discreet, prudent, self-controlled, chaste* or
> *having complete control over sensual desires.* The Greeks
> derived it from two words that mean *to keep one's mind
> safe and sound....* The one who is *sōphrōn* is in perfect
> control of every emotion and instinct, which is to say
> that the person who is *sōphrōn* is the one in whose heart
> Christ reigns supreme.[8]

You may have heard the idioms "Get a grip on yourself" and "Lock it down," meaning suck it up, deal with it, keep your emotions under control. Similarly, *sophron* means "safe mind" and refers to the ability to put one's mind in check until its proper time. I keep my guns in a fireproof gun safe. It weighs hundreds of pounds and requires a key and combination to access its contents. It is extremely difficult to move and almost as hard to open. The *sophron* man is like that. He consistently locks down his mind and makes decisions against his immediate pleasures to achieve his ultimate purpose. One's emotions, choices, and destiny are only as strong as the walls of the mind that contain them.

This sounds somehow binding or limiting, but it is quite the opposite.

PUSH-UP CHALLENGE

One year my organization, Men in the Arena, sponsored a push-up challenge where participants were invited to do 65,000 push-ups in a year. Push-ups are not difficult for most, and a person can experience rapid gains if they stick to it. The challenge was one of mental discipline more than physical strength. To hit the challenge goal, participants did either 250 push-ups five days a week or 200 six days a week. We designed a great shirt that we gave away to all the men that finished the challenge. I was initially nervous when 471 people signed up. We are a crowd-funded, nonprofit organization, and that's a lot of money to raise for shirts!

But at the end of the year, only 41 people, including yours truly, finished, and most people would not consider them the strongest men in the group. One was a twelve-year-old autistic boy who did the challenge on his own. Another shattered his wrist in a motorcycle accident and was told by doctors he would never do a push-up again. Another man was temporarily paralyzed from his waist down. To my chagrin and my wife's amusement, I needed an injection to ease my shoulder pain in order to finish. After interviewing the men who finished, we found we all had one thing in common—the discipline to reject the immediate for the ultimate.

Grit. Discipline. Mental toughness.

The disciplined man is free because he can say no to whatever he wants. True freedom is one's ability to reject the immediate to receive the ultimate. Again, a man's emotions, choices, and destiny are only as strong as the walls of the mind that contain them.

Are you getting a clearer picture of *sophron*? If we use the illustration of a gun safe and a man's mind, we get a picture of a man who not only has complete control of his present circumstances but also how those choices will affect his future—for better or worse. This is wisdom incarnate, which is why I chose "The Disciplined Man" as the chapter title. My friend Rick has one of the safest minds I know. He once told me, "I build a mote around my mind and only let certain things in." Ray Pritchard described this man as a gift: "He's a great man to have around when a tough decision needs to be made because he doesn't jump to conclusions or act solely based on emotions."[9]

Don't you envy this man?

We call this guy a gamer, and I'm not talking about video games. He is the real deal. He's mentally dialed in. He gets it done when it matters most. The *sophron* man locks down unhealthy desires and limits his choices for a better future and the best version of himself. He has learned how to control his passions and channel them accurately and decisively. He builds a mote around his mind. He keeps his mind locked up like guns in safe.

He follows sound reason and is not under the control of passion. The idea is that his desires and passions are well regulated. "The word *prudent* (in 1 Timothy 3:2) would come nearer to the meaning of the apostle than any other single word we have."[10] This man is a man of excellent understanding and has "complete *government* of all his passions."[11]

Sophron is the ability to make decisions against our immediate passions and impulses to achieve our ultimate dreams.

The man who has control over his passions is free to say no to whatever he wants and yes to what is most important. He is free to wait to take action until the timing is right. Freedom is not the right to do what you want even when it's stupid, but the ability to do as you ought. Jeremy Taylor called *sophron* "reason's girdle and passion's bridle."[12]

When I think of *sophron*, I think of decisions I make to love my wife over a lifetime. I think of choosing to father my children to be healthy adults who love Jesus, love me, and do not carry wounds from a father who neglected them in their youth. I think of being content with my finances and not getting neck-deep in debt trying to impress people I do not know or like. I think of eating and drinking with thankfulness and moderation, not being controlled by any substance. I think of keeping short accounts with anyone who has hurt or offended me, being quick to forgive and free from any man. I think of limiting my food choices to steward my body for the glory of God and prolong my life, which reminds me of a story of a man who was unable to make decisions against himself.

FREE BUT NOT REALLY

In the fourteenth century, Raynald III was a duke in what is now modern-day Belgium. Raynald's younger brother Edward successfully, violently, revolted against him. After capturing Raynald, Edward built an elaborate room surrounded by beautiful windows and doors that were always left unlocked. Edward promised his big brother that the day he left the room, his title and property would be returned to him.

But there was a catch. Not only was Raynald his big brother because of his age but also because of his size. Raynald was morbidly obese—a glutton.

Edward built doors and windows that a normal-sized human could fit through but not his big brother. Raynald needed to get to a healthy weight before he could leave the room. Knowing his older brother's gluttonous addiction to food and that he couldn't make decisions against himself, in a sick way, Edward sent his older brother delicious food every day. Lots of it. Over time, Raynald grew fatter and fatter.

But Edward maintained that he was not keeping Raynald captive: "My brother is not a prisoner. He may leave when he so wills."

And it was true.

Sort of.

Raynald stayed in that room for ten years and wasn't released until after Edward's death. By then his health was so bad that he died within a year.[13] He was in bondage to food and lost the ability to say no to it.

He lost the ability to make decisions against himself and died a lesser, albeit larger, man because of it.

Raynald's story reminds me of something my son Darby said. About three-quarters of the way up Oregon's South Sister, after having a refueling snack, I complained that my weight was limiting me substantially, and Darby in his matter-of-fact way stated, "Dad, your weight is your choice."

Enough said.

I knew the right thing to do, but I was unwilling or unable to make positive decisions against myself.

Wisdom knows the right thing to do and can choose the best path. Wisdom is more than knowledge. It is knowledge rightly acted upon. It is *sophron*. It is knowledge and making the best decisions against yourself.

Remember *sophron* comes from two Greek words that together mean "safe mind." Paul used *sophron* in Romans 12:2–3. Let's explore the context.

> And do not be conformed to this world, but be transformed by the renewing of your mind, so that you may prove what the will of God is, that which is good and acceptable and perfect.

> For through the grace given to me I say to everyone among you not to think more highly of himself than he ought to think; but to think so as to have **sound judgment** [*sophron*].

How are we nonconformists? How are we "transformed"? How do we renew our minds? How do we "prove what the will of God is"? It starts with "sound judgment," also known as *sophron*.

Making decisions according to the Bible and against yourself. That's how.

THE PROMISE

Wisdom is a journey more than a destination. A wise man today is tomorrow's fool. Like the Japanese proverb accurately states, "The reputation of a thousand years may be determined by the conduct of one hour." Wisdom is discipline (or *sophron*) compounded over time. When I think of my battle with food, lust, critical words, and poor choices, I think of the compounding effect of making the right choices over a lifetime. So many today suffer from type 2 diabetes, which has become so common that doctors are calling it "genetic," but it is often nothing more than the compounding results of wrong food choices over time.

Benjamin Franklin wrote, "After crosses and losses men grow humbler and wiser."[14] But mistakes only make us wiser if we learn to not repeat them. J. P. Moreland had this to say about wisdom: "Wisdom is also related to truth seeking. Wisdom is the wise use and application of knowledge."[15]

I've always thought it interesting how God makes so many promises in the Bible, but I can think of only one time that God promised to answer a certain prayer immediately. I have prayed one verse over more people than any other verse ever because God has promised to answer it every time: "But if any of you lacks wisdom, let him ask of God, who gives to all generously and without reproach, and it will be given to him" (James 1:5).

Not it might be or it should be, but it *will be* given to you. Now is the time to pray for wisdom. Now is the time to make decisions against yourself. I love what John Wesley once wrote, "Ought not a Minister to have, first, a good understanding, a clear apprehension, a sound judgment, and a capacity of reasoning with some closeness?"[16]

Not just minsters but all men need the wisdom to carry the weight of their full capacity. Use *sophron*. Make decisions against yourself because you see a vision of something no one else except God sees—your best version.

Don't be like Bill, the tough guy in a Cabo San Lucas bar who was bragging about his strength, conditioning, and athletic prowess. None of the regulars challenged him, but one wise and sober visitor piped up, "I'll bet you fifty bucks that I can push something in a wheelbarrow for one hundred yards along the Embarcadero, and you can't wheel it back."

Bill looked over at the skinny stranger and decided it wasn't much of a challenge. Without a second thought, he shot back, "I'll take you on!"

The two men and several regulars borrowed a fishy wheelbarrow from a local deep-sea guide service and took it to the corner. "Now, let's see what you're made of," taunted Bill.

"Okay," said the challenger. "Get in!"

Be the man who sees his future and makes decisions against himself. Be the man who makes decisions against his immediate desires to experience his ultimate best future.

DIAL IT IN
Small-Group Exercises

1. How are discipline and wisdom similar? How are they different?

2. Where are you struggling to make decisions against yourself? Who else is your struggle negatively affecting?

3. What do 1 Corinthians 9:25–27 and 2 Corinthians 10:5 teach about the power of discipline?

4. How would you define the Greek word *sophron*, literally, "safe mind"? What would it look like if you built a mote around your mind and let only certain things in?

5. Depending on the passage, the New International Version translates *sophron* as "temperate," "self-controlled," "sober," and "right mind." Other Bible translations use the word "prudent" (NASB), "sober" (KJV), "discreet" (Darby), "sensible" (HCSB), and "sober-minded" (NKJV). Which translations of *sophron* do you most resonate with, and why?

6. Based on Proverbs 16:17 and 27:12, can you think of a dangerous road you may be heading down if you don't correct your course now?

7. Read Romans 12:1–3. What do you need to offer to God as a sacrifice to live at your full capacity?

8. Share where you could use a little (or a lot) more wisdom. Take a moment and pray James 1:5 over one another.

ASSESSING YOUR CAPACITY

For each of the ten assessment statements, rank yourself accordingly:

(5) Strongly agree

(4) Agree

(3) Neither agree nor disagree

(2) Disagree

(1) Strongly disagree

Add up your total score at the bottom, then add the overall score in the appendix on page 293.

1. I am physically active at least three times a week.   _____

I do not engage in gossip or negative talk.   _____

I avoid fast food and processed foods.   _____

I get at least seven hours of sleep each night.   _____

I take at least one full day off a week.   _____

I regularly work no more than fifty hours a week.   _____

I wake up and go to bed around the same time every day. _____

I am rarely late for business or personal obligations.   _____

My weight has not fluctuated over time.   _____

I am healthy for my age.   _____

TOTAL SCORE   _____

CONCLUSION

Bastogne

We are paratroopers, Lieutenant. We are supposed to be surrounded.

—Colonel Dick Winters, *Band of Brothers*

I shall be telling this with a sigh
Somewhere ages and ages hence:
Two roads diverged in a wood, and I—
I took the one less traveled by,
And that has made all the difference.

—Robert Frost, "The Road Not Taken"

In December 1944, American units, including the 101st Airborne Division, Easy Company, famously highlighted in HBO's 2001 series *Band of Brothers*, dug in to defend the region near the Belgian town of Bastogne during what is now known as the Battle of the Bulge. It was important to the Germans because of its seven roads leading in from the Ardennes Mountains and its seven roads leading out of Bastogne.

Outnumbered five to one, without winter clothing and medical supplies and at one point down to one bullet per soldier, American troops delayed the German advance toward Bastogne, allowing American units to reach Bastogne before the German forces could surround the town and isolate it.[1]

It was a turning point in the war.

In the hit series *Band of Brothers*, which I watch annually, Easy Company was scraping any supplies they could beg, borrow, or steal from retreating American forces. This is when the supply lieutenant told Colonel Dick Winters, "Looks like you guys will be surrounded."

Winters shot back, "We are paratroopers, Lieutenant. We are supposed to be surrounded."[2]

For some of you, *Dialed In* has been an overwhelming experience. You may feel surrounded by the twenty qualities outlined in this book so that the task at hand seems overwhelming, possibly insurmountable. But you are supposed to be surrounded. Nothing could be more normal for any man who wants to live at his full capacity as a man of God.

It is critical that you honestly—brutally—answer the Assessing Your Capacity questions at the end of each chapter. Then compile your total scores in the appendix at the end of the book. Don't stop there. Input your numbers on our website (www.meninthearena.org), and see how you measure up against other men.

Then act. In Ecclesiastes 5:7, Solomon wrote simply, "Talk is cheap" (NLT). The time to get to work is after reading the book and taking the assessments. Celebrate your many strengths. I am sure you have them.

Remember, you are supposed to be surrounded. Don't panic! Focus on one quality at a time. Which one needs your immediate attention?

Continue to grow in all areas. Your goal is to be biblically qualified as a spiritual leader.

FINAL THOUGHTS ABOUT THE TWENTY

I didn't know how writing this book would impact me personally. I also didn't know what to expect when I began this project. No author does. In a way, this book is scratching my own itch. I want to be God's best version of myself. I want to be the man He crafted in my mother's womb (Ps. 139:13). I long deeply to live life at full capacity (John 10:10).

Here are a few of the finer points I'd like you to remember about the twenty qualities we discussed.

Not all of the qualities are created equal. "The Blameless Man" (chapter 1) and "The Disciplined Man" (chapter 20) bookend the rest of the chapters, with blamelessness being an umbrella over them all.

Not all men are required to become spiritual leaders, but all men should aspire to have these qualities. If a person is lacking in one or two areas, it is not the end of the world and doesn't necessarily disqualify a man from spiritual leadership permanently.

When violated, some of these qualities have weightier consequences than others. A lack of blamelessness, discipline, moderation, or faithfulness (to name a few) are immediate causes for dismissal from ministry. In churches, the consequences of such violations are up to the elders' discretion and wisdom, and restoration depends on the grace of the local church community and the betrayer's penitence.

Some of the qualities work in tandem with each other, like moderation and vigilance, protecting others and being a peacemaker, and blamelessness and discipline.

Last, some are ethical in nature, such as being blameless, respected, and calm, while others are spiritual in nature, such as being a teacher, witness, servant, and leader.

THE MAJORITY IS WRONG

I want to close by encouraging you to look up a famous picture that is widely believed to be a photo of August Landmesser in 1936 at the christening of a German destroyer. August was a shipbuilder in Nazi Germany at the time, and there is a famous photo of him in which everyone is saluting Hitler.

Everyone, except Landmesser.

The majority of Germans in the 1930s thought they were doing the right thing by going along with the Nazi agenda. The majority wins, right? As the picture testifies, Landmesser stood out in the crowd as the only one not saluting Hitler. And it cost him. He was arrested, drafted into the military, and killed in action at only thirty-four years old.

And why did he refuse? Because he was married to a Jewish woman.[3] That, my friends, is a man. He stood alone. He stood against the vast majority. He stood surrounded. He stood unashamed and unapologetically. When you commit to dialing in to your best version for Jesus, you will always be surrounded, and encouraged, by the twenty qualities we have discussed. You will also be surrounded and discouraged by an unbelieving majority that opposes any God-fearing man living out his full potential.

Do it anyway. You are a man. You are supposed to be surrounded!

NOTES

CHAPTER 1: THE BLAMELESS MAN

1 Harold Myra and Marshall Shelley, *The Leadership Secrets of Billy Graham* (Grand Rapids, MI: Zondervan, 2005), 59.

2 W. E. Vine, *An Expository Dictionary of New Testament Words* (Lynchburg, VA: Old-Time Gospel Hour, n.d.), 1185.

3 Myra and Shelley, *The Leadership Secrets of Billy Graham*, 53.

4 Frank. E. Gaebelein, ed., *The Expositor's Bible Commentary: Ephesians through Philemon* (Grand Rapids, MI: Zondervan, 1981), 364.

5 William Barclay, *Letters to Timothy, Titus, and Philemon,* The New Daily Study Bible (Louisville, KY: Westminster John Knox, 2003), 84.

6 Matthew Henry, *Matthew Henry's Commentary on the Whole Bible*, vol. 6, *Acts–Revelation* (New York: Fleming H. Revell, 1950), 815.

7 Myra and Shelley, *The Leadership Secrets of Billy Graham*, 54.

8 Josh Squires, "Sister, Friend, or Threat?", July 25, 2020, www.desiringgod.org /articles/sister-friend-or-threat.

9 Myra and Shelley, *The Leadership Secrets of Billy Graham*, 61.

CHAPTER 2: THE SERVANT

1 "The Pittsfield Streetcar Driver Who Nearly Killed Teddy Roosevelt," New England Historical Society, accessed March 18, 2024,

www.newenglandhistoricalsociety.com/the-pittsfield
-streetcar-driver-who-nearly-killed-teddy-roosevelt/

2 Candice Millard, *The River of Doubt: Theodore Roosevelt's Darkest Journey* (New York: Broadway Books, 2005), 10.

3 Millard, *The River of Doubt*, 266-67.

4 Millard, *The River of Doubt*, 265.

5 Millard, *The River of Doubt*, 267.

6 Millard, *The River of Doubt*, 280.

7 Ray Pritchard, *Man of Honor: Living the Life of Godly Character* (Wheaton, IL: Crossway, 1996), 26.

8 Albert Barnes, *Barnes' Notes: Ephesians to Philemon* (Grand Rapids, MI: Baker, 1998), 141.

9 "From the 'Letter to the Faithful' of Saint Francis of Assisi," the Holy See, accessed January 3, 2024, www.vatican.va/spirit/documents/spirit_20020203 _lettera-fedeli-2_en.html.

10 Rick Warren, *The Purpose Driven Life: What on Earth Am I Here For?* (Grand Rapids, MI: Zondervan, 2002), 262.

CHAPTER 3: THE WITNESS

1 Howard Hendricks, *Standing Together: Impacting Your Generation* (Gresham, OR: Vision House, 1995), 13.

2 Kenneth Wuest, *Wuest's Word Studies from the Greek New Testament* (Grand Rapids, MI: Eerdmans, 1966), 58.

3 James Strong, *The Exhaustive Concordance of the Bible* (Nashville, TN: Holman Bible Publishers, n.d.), 46.

4 N. T. Wright, *The Challenge of Jesus: Rediscovering Who Jesus Was and Is* (Downers Grove, IL: InterVarsity, 2015), 6.

5 Joseph Aldrich, *Gentle Persuasion: Creative Ways to Introduce Your Friends to Christ* (Portland, OR: Multnomah, 1988), 146.

6 Hendricks, *Standing Together*, 13.

CHAPTER 4: THE CALM MAN

1 "How We Made the Keep Calm and Carry On poster," *The Guardian*, April 20, 2020, www.theguardian.com/artanddesign/2020/apr/20/how-we-made-keep-calm-and-carry-on-poster.

2 William Barclay, *Letters to Timothy, Titus, and Philemon*, The New Daily Study Bible (Louisville, KY: Westminster John Knox, 2003), 266.

3 "The 5 Different Stages of Boiling Water and How the Chinese Use Them for Tea", Golden Moon Tea, accessed February 20, 2024, www.goldenmoontea.com/blogs/tea/106687623-the-5-different-stages-of-boiling-water-and-how-the-chinese-use-them-for-tea.

4 James Plath, Gail Sinclair, Kirk Curnutt, *The 100 Greatest Literary Characters* (Lanham, MD: Rowman & Littlefield, 2019), 152.

5 Barclay, *Letters to Timothy, Titus, and Philemon*, 266.

6 Gene A. Getz, *The Measure of a Man: Twenty Attributes of a Godly Man* (Grand Rapids, MI: Revell, 2016), 130.

7 "How to be Prepared for an Anaconda Attack," Preaching Today, accessed March 4, 2024, www.preachingtoday.com/illustrations/2010/december/2122710.html.

8 Red Dawn, directed by John Milius (Beverly Hills, CA: MGM, 1984).

9 Tina Hesman Saey, "Tasmanian Devils Evolve Resistance to Contagious Cancer," *Science News*, August 30, 2016, www.sciencenews.org/article/tasmanian-devils-evolve-resistance-contagious-cancer.

CHAPTER 5: THE MODERATE MAN

1 Gene A. Getz, *The Measure of a Man: Twenty Attributes of a Godly Man* (Grand Rapids, MI: Revell, 2016), 107.

2 William Barclay, *Letters to Timothy, Titus, and Philemon*, The New Daily Study Bible (Louisville, KY: Westminster John Knox, 2003), 89.

3 Matthew Henry, *Matthew Henry's Commentary on the Whole Bible*, vol. 6, *Acts–Revelation* (New York: Fleming H. Revell, 1950), 815.

4 Augustine, *Of the Good of Marriage*, New Advent, accessed January 8, 2024, www.newadvent.org/fathers/1309.htm.

CHAPTER 6: THE VIGILANT MAN

1 Albert Barnes, *Notes on the New Testament* (Grand Rapids, MI: Baker, 1998), 143.

2 Adam Clarke, *The New Testament of Our Lord and Saviour Jesus Christ* (Cincinnati: The Methodist Book Concern, 1970), 595.

3 Wayne Rice, *Hot Illustrations for Youth Talks* (El Cajon, CA: Youth Specialties, 1994), 206–07.

4 John MacArthur, *The MacArthur New Testament Commentary: 1 Timothy*, (Chicago: Moody, 1995) 106.

5 Jeff Cooper, *Principles of Personal Defense*, rev. ed. (Boulder, CO: Paladin, 2006), 14.

CHAPTER 7: THE PEACEMAKER

1 Wikipedia, "Samuel Colt," accessed March 19, 2024, https://en.wikipedia.org/wiki/Samuel_Colt.

2 Wikipedia, s.v. "Colt's Manufacturing Company," accessed March 19, 2024, https://en.wikipedia.org/wiki/Colt%27s_Manufacturing_Company.

3 Major Dan, "March 5, 1836: 'God Created Men and Sam Colt Made Them Equal!' (Old West Adage)," History & Headlines, February 17, 2020, www.historyandheadlines.com/march-5-1836-god-created-men-sam-colt-made-equalold-west-adage.

4 Ken Sande and Kevin Johnson, *Resolving Everyday Conflict* (Grand Rapids, MI: Baker, 2011).

5 Kenneth Wuest, *Wuest's Word Studies from the Greek New Testament*, vol. 2 (Grand Rapids, MI: Eerdmans, 1966), 58.

6 Robert P. Sellers, "Where Is Mike Huckabee?," Baptist News Global, April 9, 2021, https://baptistnews.com/article/where-is-mike-huckabee/.

7 Sande and Johnson, *Resolving Everyday Conflict*, 37.

8 Sande and Johnson, Resolving Everyday Conflict, 39.

9 Sande and Johnson, Resolving Everyday Conflict, 41.

10 Rick Warren, *The Purpose Driven Life: What on Earth Am I Here For?* (Grand Rapids, MI: Zondervan, 2002), 154 (emphasis in the original).

11 Sande and Johnson, *Resolving Everyday Conflict,* 37.

12 Sande and Johnson, *Resolving Everyday Conflict*, 43.

13 Dietrich Bonhoeffer, *Life Together: The Classic Exploration of Christian Community*, trans. John W. Doberstein (New York: Harper One, 1954), 107.

CHAPTER 8: THE PROTECTOR

1 Christian Reisner, *Roosevelt's Religion* (Cincinnati: Abingdon Press, 1922), 324.

2 Source TK.

3 Paul Coughlin, *Free Us from Bullying: Real Solutions beyond Being Nice* (Abilene, TX: Leafwood Publishers, 2018), 7.

4 Dale L. June, *Fear, Society, and the Police* (New York, NY: Taylor & Francis, 2019).

5 John MacArthur, *The MacArthur New Testament Commentary: Matthew 1–7* (Chicago: Moody, 1985), 329.

6 Paul Coughlin, *Free Us from Bullying: Real Solutions beyond Being Nice* (Abilene, TX: Leafwood Publishers, 2018), 18.

CHAPTER 9: THE HOSPITABLE MAN

1 *Wikipedia*, s.v. "Pashtunwali," accessed March 18, 2024, https://en.wikipedia.org/wiki/Pashtunwali.

2 Ray Pritchard, *Man of Honor: Living the Life of Godly Character* (Wheaton, IL: Crossway, 1996), 126.

3 John MacArthur, *The MacArthur New Testament Commentary: 1 Timothy* (Chicago: Moody, 1995), 107.

4 Henri J. M. Nouwen, *Reaching Out: The Three Movements of the Spiritual Life* (New York: Doubleday, 1975), 71.

5 Gene A. Getz, *The Measure of a Man: Twenty Attributes of a Godly Man* (Grand Rapids, MI: Revell, 2016), 91.

CHAPTER 10: THE GENEROUS MAN

1 Leonardo Blair, "Only 13% of Evangelicals Tithe, Half Give Away Less Than 1% of Income Annually: Study," Christian Post, October 29, 2021, www.christianpost.com/news/only-13-of-evangelicals-tithe-study.html.

2 Charles White, "What Wesley Practiced and Preached About Money," *Mission Frontiers*, September 1,1994, www.missionfrontiers.org/issue/article /what-wesley-practiced-and-preached-about-money.

3 Ken Sloane, "'The Use of Money' by John Wesley," Discipleship Ministries, The United Methodist Church, accessed January 10, 2024, www.umcdiscipleship.org/articles/the-use-of-money-by-john-wesley.

4 "Peace Prayer," Loyola Press, accessed January 8, 2024, www.loyolapress.com/catholic-resources/prayer/traditional -catholic-prayers/saints-prayers/peace-prayer-of-saint-francis/.

5 W. E. Vine, *An Expository Dictionary of New Testament Words* (Lynchburg, VA: Old-Time Gospel Hour, n.d.), 695.

6 John MacArthur, *The MacArthur New Testament Commentary: 1 Timothy* (Chicago: Moody, 1985), 112.

7 Ray Pritchard, *Man of Honor: Living the Life of Godly Character* (Wheaton, IL: Crossway, 1996), 236.

CHAPTER 11: THE GOOD MAN

1 *Saving Private Ryan*, directed by Steven Spielberg (Paramount Pictures, 1998), DVD.

2 *Saving Private Ryan*, 1998, DVD.

3 *Saving Private Ryan*, 1998, DVD.

4 Henry David Thoreau, *Walden* (London: George Routledge & Sons, 1904), 179.

5 "What Does 'Nice' Mean, Anyway?" Merriam-Webster, accessed January 4, 2024, www.merriam-webster.com/wordplay/nice-multiple-meanings.

6 Brennan Manning, *The Ragamuffin Gospel* (Colorado Springs: Multnomah, 2005), 147.

7 Paul Coughlin, *No More Christian Nice Guy: Why Being Nice—Instead of Good—Hurts Men, Women, and Children* (Minneapolis: Bethany House, 2005), 17.

8 Coughlin, *No More Christian Nice Guy*, 22 (emphasis added).

9 Martin Luther King Jr., "Address at the Fourth Annual Institute on Nonviolence and Social Change at Bethel Baptist Church," Stanford University, accessed March 18, 2024, https://kinginstitute.stanford.edu

/king-papers/documents/address-fourth-annual-institute-nonviolence -and-social-change-bethel-baptist.

10 William Barclay, *The Letters to Timothy, Titus, and Philemon,* The New Study Bible (Louisville: Westminster John Knox, 2003), 268 (emphasis mine).

11 W. E. Vine, *An Expository Dictionary of New Testament Words* (Lynchburg, VA: Old-Time Gospel Hour, n.d.), 493.

12 Kenny Luck, *Dangerous Good: The Coming Revolution of Men Who Care* (Colorado Springs: NavPress, 2018), 8.

13 William Barclay, *The Letters to Timothy, Titus, and Philemon* (Louisville, KY: Westminster John Knox, 2003), 268.

14 C. S. Lewis, *The Lion, the Witch and the Wardrobe* (New York: Harper Trophy, 1950), 79–80.

15 Theodore Roosevelt, *Theodore Roosevelt: An Autobiography* (New York: Macmillan, 1913), 96.

16 John Eldredge, *Wild at Heart: Discovering the Secret of a Man's Soul* (Nashville, TN: Thomas Nelson, 2010), 24 (emphasis in original).

CHAPTER 12: THE DEVOUT MAN

1 E. M. Bounds, *The Essentials of Prayer* (Dallas: Gideon House, 2016), 84.

2 Gary Thomas, *The Authentic Faith: The Power of a Fire-Tested Life* (Grand Rapids, MI: Zondervan, 2002), 113 (emphasis in original).

3 Bounds, *The Essentials of Prayer,* 10.

4 Rick Vance, "Lessons from John Wesley," United Methodist Men, March 29, 2021, www.gcumm.org/news/lessons-from-john-wesley/.

5 Albert Barnes, *Notes on the New Testament* (Grand Rapids, MI: Baker, 1998), 269.

6 Oxford Learner's Dictionaries, s.v. "devout (adj.)," accessed February 23, 2024, www.oxfordlearnersdictionaries.com/definition/english/devout.

7 W. E. Vine, *An Expository Dictionary of New Testament Words* (Lynchburg, VA: Old-Time Gospel Hour, n.d.), 557.

8 Frank. E. Gaebelein, ed., *The Expositor's Bible Commentary: Ephesians through Philemon* (Grand Rapids, MI: Zondervan, 1981), 431.

9 Jerry Bridges, *The Practice of Godliness* (Colorado Springs: NavPress, 1983), 149.

10 J. Oswald Sanders, "Maturity Can Be Measured, *Knowing and Doing*, C. S. Lewis Institute, December 1, 2005, https://www.cslewisinstitute.org/wp-content/uploads/KD-2005-Winter-Growing-in-Christ-Maturity-Can-Be-Measured-627.pdf.

11 Vine, *An Expository Dictionary of New Testament Words*, 1247.

12 Patrick Morley, David Delk, and Brett Clemmer, No Man Left Behind: How to Build and Sustain a Thriving Disciple-Making Ministry for Every Man in Your Church (Chicago: Moody, 2006), 47.

CHAPTER 13: THE RESPECTED MAN

1 Aretha Franklin, vocalist, "Respect," by Otis Redding, track 1 on *I Never Loved a Man the Way I Love You*, Atlantic Records, 1967.

2 "The 500 Greatest Songs of All Time," Rolling Stone, September 15, 2021, www.rollingstone.com/music/music-lists/best-songs-of-all-time-1224767/.

3 Rolling Stone, "500 Greatest Songs."

4 William Barclay, *Letters to Timothy, Titus, and Philemon*, The New Daily Study Bible (Louisville, KY: Westminster John Knox, 2003), 90–91.

5 Barclay, *Letters to Timothy, Titus, and Philemon*, 91.

6 John C. Maxwell, *The 21 Irrefutable Laws of Leadership* (Nashville, TN: Thomas Nelson, 1998), 61.

7 Bill Perkins, *6 Rules Every Man Must Break* (Carol Stream, IL: Tyndale, 2007), 88.

CHAPTER 14: THE SACRIFICIAL MAN

1 *Hacksaw Ridge*, directed by Mel Gibson (Santa Monica, CA: Summit Entertainment, 2017), DVD.

2 Lisa Taylor, "'Hacksaw Ridge' Biopic Commemorates Selfless Service of Desmond Doss," Folklife Today: American Folklife Center & Veterans History Project (blog), Library of Congress, August 30, 2016, https://blogs.loc.gov/folklife/2016/08/hacksaw-ridge-biopic-commemorates-selfless-service-of-desmond-doss/.

3 Rick Warren, *The Purpose Driven Life: What on Earth Am I Here For?* (Grand Rapids, MI: Zondervan, 2002), 21.

4 "General Particulars of Steamship 'Titanic,'" U. S. Senate Inquiry Report, accessed March 4, 2024, www.titanicinquiry.org/USInq/USReport /AmInqRep03.php#a7.

5 Kenneth Wuest, *Wuest's Word Studies from the Greek New Testament*, vol. 2 (Grand Rapids, MI: Eerdmans, 1966), 184.

6 W. E. Vine, *An Expository Dictionary of New Testament Words* (Lynchburg, VA: Old-Time Gospel Hour, n.d.), 1014.

7 Matthew Henry, *Matthew Henry's Commentary on the Whole Bible*, vol. 6, *Acts–Revelation* (New York: Fleming H. Revell, 1950), 857.

8 William Barclay, *Letters to Timothy, Titus, and Philemon*, The New Daily Study Bible (Louisville, KY: Westminster John Knox, 2003), 265.

9 Barclay, *Letters to Timothy, Titus, and Philemon*, 265.

CHAPTER 15: THE LEADER

1 David Legge, "Back to Basics—Part 12: 'Assurance,'" Preach the Word, April 2005, www.preachtheword.com/sermon/b2b12.shtml.

2 LeRoy Eims, *Be the Leader You Were Meant to Be: Lessons on Leadership from the Bible* (Colorado Springs: David C Cook, 1975), 86.

3 Kenneth Wuest, *Wuest's Word Studies from the Greek New Testament* (Grand Rapids, MI: Eerdmans, 1966), 557.

4 John MacArthur, *The MacArthur New Testament Commentary: 1 Timothy* (Chicago: Moody, 1985), 116.

5 Franklin D. Roosevelt, "Address at University of Pennsylvania," The American Presidency Project, accessed March 4, 2024, www.presidency .ucsb.edu/node/210464.

6 James C. Dobson, *The Strong-Willed Child: Birth through Adolescence*, (Carol Stream, IL: Tyndale, 1992), 245–46.

CHAPTER 16: THE TEACHER

1 I was on a prayer walk in 1989 when God spoke Psalm 45:2 to my heart. I didn't even know it was in the Bible at the time!

2 William Barclay, *Letters to Timothy, Titus, and Philemon*, The New Daily Study Bible (Louisville, KY: Westminster John Knox, 2003), 93.

3 John MacArthur, *The MacArthur New Testament Commentary: 1 Timothy* (Chicago: Moody, 1985), 108.

4 Gene A. Getz, *The Measure of a Man: Twenty Attributes of a Godly Man* (Grand Rapids, MI: Revell, 2016), 99.

5 Merriam-Webster, s.v. "didactic," accessed November 26, 2023, www.merriam-webster.com/dictionary/didactic.

6 Ray Pritchard, *Man of Honor: Living the Life of Godly Character* (Wheaton, IL: Crossway, 1996), 185.

7 Adam Clarke, *The New Testament of Our Lord and Saviour Jesus Christ* (Cincinnati: The Methodist Book Concern, 1970), 595.

8 Matthew Henry, *Matthew Henry's Commentary on the Whole Bible*, vol. 6, *Acts–Revelation* (New York: Fleming H. Revell, 1950), 515 (emphasis added).

9 Tim Challies, "Counterfeit Detection (Part 1)," Challies (blog), June 27, 2006, www.challies.com/articles/counterfeit-detection-part-1/.

10 Wayne Rice, *Hot Illustrations for Youth Talks: 100 Attention-Getting Stories, Parables, and Anecdotes* (El Cajon, CA: Youth Specialties, 1994), 165–66.

11 Rice, *Hot Illustrations for Youth Talks*, 166.

CHAPTER 17: THE FAITHFUL MAN

1 William Barclay, *Letters to Timothy, Titus, and Philemon*, The New Daily Study Bible (Louisville, KY: Westminster John Knox, 2003), 87.

2 Barclay, *Letters to Timothy, Titus, and Philemon*, 87.

3 Barclay, *Letters to Timothy, Titus, and Philemon*, 85–86.

4 C. S. Lewis, *The Collected Letters of C. S. Lewis*, ed. *Walter Hooper*, vol. 3 (New York: HarperCollins, 2007), 1954.

5 Gene A. Getz, *The Measure of a Man: Twenty Attributes of a Godly Man* (Grand Rapids, MI: Revell, 2016), 40.

6 Merriam-Webster, s.v. "lust," accessed January 9, 2024, www.merriam-webster.com/dictionary/lust.

7 Jim Ramos, *The Trailhead: Protecting Integrity, Strong Men Series Study Guide* (Dallas: Five Stones, 2021) 56–57.

CHAPTER 18: THE JUST MAN

1 Charles R. Swindoll, *Living above the Level of Mediocrity* (Dallas: World Publishing, 1989).

2 W. E. Vine, *An Expository Dictionary of New Testament Words* (Lynchburg, VA: Old-Time Gospel Hour, n.d.), 969.

3 "1342. Dikaios," Thayer's Greek Lexicon, accessed March 5, 2024, https://biblehub.com/greek/1342.htm.

4 William Barclay, *Letters to Timothy, Titus, and Philemon*, The New Daily Study Bible (Louisville, KY: Westminster John Knox, 2003), 269.

5 Albert Barnes, *Notes on the New Testament* (Grand Rapids, MI: Baker Books, 1998), 269.

6 Wikipedia, s.v. "Zaleucus," last modified July 22, 2023, https://en.wikipedia.org/wiki/Zaleucus.

7 "Read Martin Luther King Jr.'s 'I Have a Dream' Speech in Its Entirety," NPR, January 16, 2023, www.npr.org/2010/01/18/122701268/i-have-a-dream-speech-in-its-entirety.

8 Wikipedia, s.v. "Knights Templar," accessed March 9, 2024, https://en.wikipedia.org/wiki/Knights_Templar#CITEREFBarber1992.

9 "Eulogy on Mr. Justice Story," *Select Speeches of Daniel Webster*, Project Gutenberg, accessed February 29, 2024, www.gutenberg.org/files/7600/7600-h/7600-h.htm.

CHAPTER 19: THE GENTLE MAN

1 Wess Stafford, "Living with Passion," July 8, 2017, *Men in the Arena*, podcast, episode 48, produced by Men in the Arena, https://podcast.meninthearena.org/48-living-with-passion-w-wess-stafford/

2 Jonathan Edwards quoted in Gary Thomas, *The Glorious Pursuit: Becoming Who God Created Us to Be* (Colorado Springs: NavPress, 1998), 172.

3 William Barclay, *Letters to Timothy, Titus, and Philemon*, The New Daily Study Bible: (Louisville, KY: Westminster John Knox, 2003), 93.

4 Barclay, *Letters to Timothy, Titus, and Philemon*, 93 (emphasis added).

5 Jerry Bridges, *The Practice of Godliness* (Colorado Springs: NavPress, 1983), 220.

6 Brennan Manning, *The Ragamuffin Gospel* (Colorado Springs: Multnomah, 2005), 55.

7 Bridges, *The Practice of Godliness*, 222.

8 Paul Eldridge, *Maxims for a Modern Man* (United States: T. Yoseloff, 1965) 143.

CHAPTER 20: THE DISCIPLINED MAN

1 Wikipedia, s.v. "prudence," last modified November 8, 2023, https://en.wikipedia.org/wiki/Prudence.

2 Merriam-Webster, s.v. "prudence," accessed January 9, 2024, www.merriam-webster.com/dictionary/prudence.

3 Stephen R. Covey, *The 7 Habits of Highly Effective People: Powerful Lessons in Personal Change* (New York: Free Press, 1989), 97.

4 Henry Cloud, *9 Things You Simply Must Do to Succeed in Love and Life* (Nashville, TN: Thomas Nelson, 2004), 69.

5 Dave Ramsey, *The Total Money Makeover: A Proven Plan for Financial Fitness* (Nashville, TN: Thomas Nelson, 2009), 5 (emphasis added).

6 Wayne Rice, *Hot Illustrations for Youth Talks: 100 Attention-Getting Stories, Parables, and Anecdotes* (Grand Rapids, MI: Zondervan, 1986), 174.

7 Kenneth Wuest, *Wuest's Word Studies from the Greek New Testament*, vol. 2 (Grand Rapids, MI: Eerdmans, 1966), 55.

8 William Barclay, *Letters to Timothy, Titus, and Philemon*, The New Daily Study Bible (Louisville, KY: Westminster John Knox, 2003), 89 (emphasis added).

9 Ray Pritchard, *Man of Honor: Living the Life of Godly Character* (Wheaton, IL: Crossway, 1996), 44.

10 Albert Barnes, *Notes on the New Testament* (Grand Rapids, MI: Baker, 1998), 143.

11 Adam Clarke, *The New Testament of Our Lord and Saviour Jesus Christ* (Cincinnati: The Methodist Book Concern, 1970), 595.

12 Barclay, *Letters to Timothy, Titus, and Philemon*, 90.

13 "Prisoner of His Appetite," Ministry127, accessed January 9, 2024, https://ministry127.com/resources/illustration/prisoner-of-his-appetite.

14 Benjamin Franklin, *The Autobiography of Benjamin Franklin* (New York: American Book, 1896), 198.

15 J. P. Moreland, *Love Your God with All Your Mind: The Role of Reason in the Life of the Soul*, rev. ed. (Colorado Springs: NavPress, 2012).

16 John Wesley, *The Works of the Rev. John Wesley, A.M., Sometime Fellow of Lincoln College, Oxford*, 4th ed., vol. 10 (London: John Mason, 1841), 462.

CONCLUSION

1 Wikipedia, s.v. "Battle of the Bulge," last modified December 31, 2023, https://en.wikipedia.org/wiki/Battle_of_the_Bulge.

2 *Band of Brothers*, episode 5, "Cross Roads," directed by Tom Hanks, written by Erik Jendresen, aired 2001 on HBO.

3 Wikipedia, s.v. "August Landmesser," last modified September 30, 2023, https://en.wikipedia.org/wiki/August_Landmesser.

ACKNOWLEDGMENTS

I want to thank several men for making this project happen. First, I want to thank my friend, great author, and mentor Bill Perkins for being available to equip and inspire me back when I was sorting out my call to men's ministry. When others blew me off, he leaned into what God was preparing in me. He continues to run hard after Jesus.

I want to acknowledge John Eldredge for his classic *Wild at Heart*, which I have read a half dozen times and quote to this day. It continues to inspire the way I connect with men through the written word.

I want to acknowledge two authors (I know of) who published similar works that inspired this one. In 1974 Pastor Gene Getz published *The Measure of a Man*. Then in 1996, Ray Pritchard released his book titled *Man of Honor*. Both works focused on the call to masculinity from the Pastoral Epistles, which I referenced throughout this project.

I want to thank the board members who offered their wisdom, sweat equity, and advice on this project: Mike Goins, Gary McCusker (my spiritual father), John Kent (who crafted the Assessing Your Capacity sections), Kai Munshi, Pat George, and Jeff Dyck.

Last, I want to thank my high school English teacher Bruce Badrigian for inspiring me to be a better writer in 1984.

APPENDIX

Dialed In *Assessment Scores*

Copy below the scores you wrote at the end of each chapter, and then add them up to learn your Dialed In total score. When complete, visit our website, meninthearena.org/dialedinscores, to enter your total score for more resources.

Chapter 1: The Blameless Man   SCORE: _____

Chapter 2: The Servant   SCORE: _____

Chapter 3: The Witness   SCORE: _____

Chapter 4: The Calm Man   SCORE: _____

Chapter 5: The Moderate Man   SCORE: _____

Chapter 6: The Vigilant Man   SCORE: _____

Chapter 7: The Peacemaker   SCORE: _____

Chapter 8: The Protector   SCORE: _____

Chapter 9: The Hospitable Man   SCORE: _____

Chapter 10: The Generous Man   SCORE: _____

Chapter 11: The Good Man   SCORE: _____

Chapter 12: The Devout Man   SCORE: _____

Chapter 13: The Respected Man   SCORE: _____

Chapter 14: The Sacrificial Man   SCORE: _____

Chapter 15: The Leader   SCORE: _____

Chapter 16: The Teacher   SCORE: _____

Chapter 17: The Faithful Man   SCORE: _____

Chapter 18: The Just Man   SCORE: _____

Chapter 19: The Gentle Man   SCORE   SCORE: _____

Chapter 20: The Disciplined Man   SCORE: _____

                                           TOTAL: _____

To find out where you stand as a dialed in man, visit www.menint-hearena.org/dialedinscore or scan this QR code to enter your score on our website and access more resources.

ABOUT THE AUTHOR

Jim is a nationally sought-after keynote speaker, bestselling author, and internationally known podcaster whose passionate exposition of God's Word, relational humor, and epic storytelling skills will keep you on the edge of your seat.

He has written many books, including *Guts and Manhood: Four Irrefutable Attributes of Courage*, *The Field Guide: A Bathroom Book for Men*, Strong Men Study Guide series, and the Amazon number one bestseller *Strong Men Dangerous Times: Five Essentials Every Man Must Possess to Change His World*.

Jim lives in McMinnville, Oregon, with his flight attendant bride since 1992, Shanna. His goal is to live each day to its fullest with courageous abandon. When not ministering to men, he is passionate about hunting with his three adult sons; fly-fishing the Lower Deschutes River from their place near Maupin, Oregon; taking tropical vacations; and listening to men share their stories over a café Americano.

To share your hero story of transformation, contact Jim at info@menin-thearena.org.